The Coach's Guide to Mind Mapping

I dedicate this book to the memory of Mandy Croston who was a loved and valued colleague and one of the best coach educators I know.

– Misia Gervis

I dedicate this book to my Father in Heaven who through Him all things are and continue to be possible; to my dear wife Adura who encouraged me and was never unwavering in her support in spite of the regular late nights and long weekends away; and to my remarkably supportive family, friends, and ISOG who relentlessly cheered me on. God bless you all.

–Temisan Williams

MISIA GERVIS
TEMISAN WILLIAMS

THE COACH'S
GUIDE
TO MIND MAPPING

THE FUNDAMENTAL TOOLS TO
BECOME AN EXPERT COACH AND MAXIMIZE
YOUR PLAYERS' PERFORMANCE

Meyer & Meyer Sport

British Library Cataloguing in Publication Data

A catalogue record for this book is available from the British Library

The Coach's Guide to Mind Mapping

Maidenhead: Meyer & Meyer Sport (UK) Ltd., 2017

ISBN: 978-1-78255-119-5

© 2017 by Meyer & Meyer Sport (UK) Ltd.

Aachen, Auckland, Beirut, Cairo, Cape Town, Dubai, Hägendorf, Hong Kong, Indianapolis, Manila, New Delhi, Singapore, Sydney, Tehran, Vienna

 Member of the World Sport Publishers' Association (WSPA)

Manufacturing: Print Consult GmbH, Munich, Germany

ISBN: 978-1-78255-119-5

Email: info@m-m-sports.com

www.m-m-sports.com

CONTENTS

LIST OF TABLES AND FIGURES

PREFACE

This book is the culmination of a number of years of conversations, exploration, and lived experience between a sport psychologist and a soccer coach. This collaboration has brought together the experiences of the coach educator and soccer practitioner as a response to the real problem, that of enhancing on-the-job learning for coaches. Through both of our unique perspectives we have endeavoured to create a book that uses current scientific knowledge about expertise and applies it in a new context using the techniques of mind mapping.

ABOUT THE BOOK

As a modern-day coach, trying to balance the vast expectations and responsibilities is hard enough, let alone trying to track, measure, and develop your own learning and coaching skills. In a bid to empower coaches from all walks of life, we wanted to use a well-known cognitive technique, mind mapping, as a powerful learning tool to develop your expertise. In spite of the many areas exploring the mind-mapping technique to develop business strategies and effective teams and for personal cognitive growth, surprisingly this technique has not been widely used within the soccer family and the larger sporting world. Moreover, at first glance, you might be wondering what the connection between mind mapping and developing expertise is. However, they are not only connected but also intertwined in their impact for self-development. Fundamentally, it's a simple equation:

Knowing myself + Knowing what I need to develop + Having the tools to develop
= Increasing expertise and coaching impact

Unfortunately, the key elements of this sum are not maximized or engaged in to a consistent and competent level. This causes coaches to waste precious time developing the skills needed to progress their level of expertise. Indeed, it has become somewhat of a craze for soccer coaches to place an extreme emphasis on acquiring session plan upon session plan while largely neglecting the intricacies of communication or their level of emotional intelligence, which are both hallmarks of expert coaches. Consequently, this book deliberately doesn't provide the reader with outlines of session plans, but rather explores the steps for self-assessment within the development of expertise spectrum.

Although soccer examples are used throughout the book, the information and techniques within the book are applicable to coaches across a variety of sports. It is anticipated that although coaches who pick up this book will have a wide range of experiences, the principles remain transferable across the coaching spectrum. The book is deliberately written in a coach reader-friendly manner to help you to navigate through each chapter with ease and clarity. Examples are provided where necessary and to provide reference points for coaches when practicing the techniques.

Fundamentally, this book intends to present new and interactive ways for you to develop expertise as a coach.

ACKNOWLEDGMENTS

We would like to thank some important people who have helped us in the development and production of this book. Without their considerable help and support we would not have been able to bring this project to fruition. First we would like to thank Chris Ramsey and Jim Hicks who offered their extensive knowledge and expertise of football coaching education to us which proved to be invaluable. We also thank Rashid Abba who was really helpful in offering key advice in relation to the mind maps. Further gratitude goes to Lisanne Radice, Giles Radice, and Emily Hayday for all their excellent help in editing and proofreading. We appreciate all your efforts on our behalf.

Acknowledgments

INTRODUCTION

HOW TO MIND MAP YOUR WAY TO BECOMING AN EXPERT COACH

Fundamentally, the job of a coach is to develop players across a season, generally through training sessions and games. So the question is how do you maximize your time for the benefit of your players and develop expertise as a coach?

Difficult question! Agreed. Then let's debunk the myth and appreciate that coaching is difficult and requires a range of finely tuned skills, many of which are undervalued. Becoming a successful coach is not simply about understanding the game, it is about being able to plan, communicate effectively, understand individual needs, and much more besides.

With so many aspects of coaching to consider, trying to organize the complex process can prove to be both challenging and confusing. Whether you are working at the elite or grassroots level of the game, knowing the what, why, when, and how of the coaching process doesn't come easily! Coaches need all the help they can get and the purpose of this book is to provide you with a set of tools that will enable you to develop better, faster, and more effectively.

The key to doing this is to learn how to mind map.

Mind mapping has traditionally been used in a variety of non-sporting contexts such as business and education. However, as a powerful self-directed learning technique, its benefits can be universally applied within any sporting context and are accessible to coaches undertaking any sporting qualification. Throughout this book you will be introduced to the mind-mapping process as an interactive coach-learning tool. This book is intended to be deliberately different. Most of the coaching literature available today places an emphasis on acquiring knowledge through session plans and coaching courses. However, this approach doesn't recognise or understand who you are, what your needs are, the context you are working in, or the demands of your club. In essence it's a one-size-fits-all approach and creates limitations in developing yourself as a professional. Therefore this book focuses on developing how you—the coach—can:

- Accurately evaluate your current coaching skills
- Understand your own soccer memory bank
- Enhance, develop, and acquire specific coaching expertise
- Identify your personal strengths in order to support the development of your expertise
- Advance your reflective practice skills
- Apply these principles to those you are coaching

THE TRADITIONAL LEARNING JOURNEY

As part of the archetypal coach's journey, access to formal coaching qualifications through National Soccer Associations plays a significant role. Many coaches expect to develop fundamental expertise by acquiring these formal coaching qualifications. However, research by Cushion, Armour, and Jones (2003) shows that only a limited amount (approximately 10%) of meaningful learning takes place on coaching courses. In other words 90% of a coach's knowledge is acquired on the job. Understandably, the mindset of most coaches on a course is "I'm here to learn." They will therefore participate in the learning activities embedded in the course and take on new information. However, the real challenge is how to ensure that coaches actively translate what they have learned on the course into their everyday coaching practice. What the evidence tells us is that new information is quickly forgotten and the benefits are only short term.

So the question is, what is happening with the other 90% of a coach's informal learning? This process usually lacks clear direction and depth of purpose, and is essentially chaotic as coaches may not even be aware of the personal learning taking place. It is essential that informal learning becomes more purposeful and effective. Furthermore, with many coaches engaging in more coach education courses, continued professional development, and training experiences than before, the process of effective formal learning is also increasingly important.

But, here's the underlying issue: many coaches find the ability to organise, remember, and recall new information a challenging process. One of the key characteristics of the expert coach involves the advancement of not only their knowledge base, but also how they apply it. Of course, we recognize that the challenge faced by many adult learners is that they are struggling to develop the required expertise as well as understand their own ways of learning. Hence, this book is designed to help you with both informal and formal learning in order to maximize the opportunities to develop your expertise and become a better and more effective coach.

HOW TO USE THIS RESOURCE

This book is designed to be an interactive coaching tool which requires you to participate actively in the process. You will be able to practice skills, reflect on your practice and develop your learning strategies. Throughout this program you will develop self-awareness, which is at the cornerstone of self-development and improvement. The book is divided into five main chapters, which are:

- The Mind-Mapping Process
- Developing Expertise
- Developing Your Coaching Strengths
- Reflective Practice Skills
- Application of Purposeful Practice for your Players

The Mind-Mapping Process

In the first chapter, you will be introduced to the mind-mapping process and presented with step-by-step guidelines for developing, creating, and evaluating the impact of the mind-mapping technique. Common soccer topics (such as principles of play and playing out from the back) are used to help you follow the mind-mapping examples with ease. There will be simple interactive activities which will help you practice and develop the mind-mapping technique. Here you will also acquire an understanding of how to remember and recall technical coaching information and formulate coaching points for specific session topics.

Developing Expertise

Following the mind-mapping process, you will learn about Dreyfus' model outlining the five stages of development from a novice to an expert. This chapter explores the critical science on how to develop expertise and offers applied solutions to enhance your development. You will also be introduced to the concept of purposeful practice, which is a way of enhancing your learning in informal settings.

Developing Your Coaching Strengths

In general, many people find it difficult to identify their strengths and how they can use them to enhance personal development, skill acquisition, and expert characteristics. This is no different for coaches, so this chapter will support your ability to identify, assess, and use your strengths and qualities.

Reflective Practice Skills

Chapter 4 explores a theme which, although of broad and current interest in the coaching arena, remains either inadequately understood or is implemented only on a superficial level. Undoubtedly, the ability to effectively reflect is a principal skill of an expert coach. While the concept of reflection is common, rarely do coaches get taught how to do it.

Application of Purposeful Practice for Your Players

The final chapter shows you how to apply the principles of purposeful practice within your coaching context to ensure that your players are given the opportunity to maximize their development of expertise. In other words, you can use the same principles to develop your players.

"My extraordinary experience and immediate personal success led me to realize that mind maps could be developed as a powerful tool for personal transformation and as a way for each of us to make the most of our natural abilities."

Tony Buzan
Founder of mind mapping

MASTERING THE TECHNIQUE OF MIND MAPPING

1.1 THE SCIENCE BEHIND MIND MAPPING: WHY IT WORKS

A well-known method for creatively organising and linking both related and supposedly unrelated information is via the mind-mapping process. Mind mapping was pioneered and developed in the 1960s by Tony Buzan, and has been used across a variety of sectors, but remains largely underused as an effective learning tool in the soccer coaching domain. Through this unique, organised brainstorming system, the mind-mapping technique focuses on improving the functioning of the brain. While the left side of the brain manages logic and analytical data, creative thinking is located in the right side of the brain. The uniqueness of mind mapping is that it provides the opportunity for the right and left sides of the brain to talk to each other, thus maximizing the possibility for formulating new concepts and understanding.

Imagine you are driving down a road and arrive at a junction with multiple options. The signs inform you of the direction for the different towns which you could drive toward. You take the road to your left, but along that route you notice another sign which tells you if you turn right, you can drive along a road that will take you to one of the towns you saw on the signs at the junction. You have made a brand new and unexpected route or connection! Similarly, in a coaching sense, your focus for your team might be switching play. Now this could be achieved in one pass, two passes, three passes, and so on. With each additional pass an extra player or movement is involved which then extends the potential possibilities and ideas as to how you can achieve switching play. Ultimately, the mind-mapping technique relies upon the coach to draw upon their own experience to connect and creatively organize pre-existing information into something new. As new concepts are formed from pre-existing knowledge, the ability to recall coaching information from memory gradually becomes increasingly automated. Through organizing our thoughts with the help of a mind map, our ability to develop expertise is greatly enhanced.

Indeed, nowadays, knowledge and its effective application are considered to be at the heart of coach development. An extensive knowledge base is recognized as a prime requirement of an expert.

One of the main reasons why coaches historically failed to fulfill the UEFA B final assessment criteria was due to their inability to develop and apply their knowledge in practice.

Overall the mind-mapping technique is beneficial for several purposes, including:

- Summarizing information
- Brainstorming (independently or as a group)
- Quick note taking
- Content creation

- Formation of ideas or concepts
- Problem solving
- Rapid thought recording
- Planning
- Introspection and self-awareness

Whether the mind map is used for summarizing information, for problem solving, or for rapid thought recording, it eventually leads the coach to have more meaningful and self-regulated learning. This has been summarized by education experts Paris and Paris (2001) who, when discussing self-regulated learning, said that this "emphasises autonomy and control by the individual who monitors, directs and regulates actions towards goals of information acquisition, expanding expertise and self-improvement."

To make sure that you experience the advantages of using the mind-mapping technique, it will be essential to set aside small but regular periods of time to develop your learning. Whether it's 10 minutes a day or 30 minutes at the beginning of each week, enjoy becoming familiar with the mind-mapping technique, identifying your qualities as a coach, and developing coaching expertise.

So go ahead—Learn, Coach, Grow!

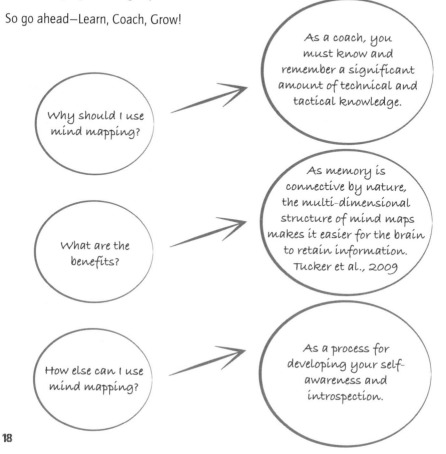

Why should I use mind mapping?

As a coach, you must know and remember a significant amount of technical and tactical knowledge.

What are the benefits?

As memory is connective by nature, the multi-dimensional structure of mind maps makes it easier for the brain to retain information. Tucker et al., 2009

How else can I use mind mapping?

As a process for developing your self-awareness and introspection.

1.2 HOW TO CONSTRUCT A MIND MAP

The central topic is placed in the center of the page, surrounded by a bubble or used as an image. The main sub-topics are then positioned on the outside of the central topic, linked via connecting lines. From these sub-topics, key words, ideas, and phrases branch off.

Different colors can then be used to represent the different sub-topics and related information in a four-stage process (see table 1):

1. Central topic
2. Sub-topic
3. Branches
4. Extended detail

Central Topic

This is the main theme of the mind map, which is usually broad (e.g., attacking, defending, passing). The central position of the main theme enables the fluid flow of information to produce the mind map.

Sub-Topic

These are the main topics, which are directly related to the central topic (e.g., attacking in wide areas, defending with a deep block, or long passing). These are also referred to as the basic ordering ideas (BOI) to guide the concepts in the branches and sub-branches.

Branches

A variety of more specific areas extend from the sub-topics. These are the main concepts within the sub-topic and reveal an additional level of information.

Sub-Branches

Additional branches are added to further enhance the information within the sub-topic to extend a greater depth of detail. It's important to note that there is no limit to the number of sub-branches you can create.

Table 1 Example of mind-map information

Central topic	Principles of play
Sub-topic 1	Attacking principles of play
Branches	Dispersal, improvisation, movement, penetration, support
Sub-branches	Angles, around, between, centrally, combinations, distances, group, height, individual, laterally, over, through, width
Sub-topic 2	Defensive principles of play
Branches	Balance, concentration, control and restraint, delay and deny, depth
Sub-branches	Angle of support, compactness, counterattack, distances, marking, patience, predictability, pressing, restricting space, unit shape

Color Coordinating

As part of the mind-mapping process, it's important to use color coding for each topic. Research has shown that "colour draws on both the symbolic and cognitive powers to affect learning, facilitating memorisation and identification of concept" (Olurinola and Tayo, 2015). This is due to the color-processing power of the right side of the brain, which in turn enhances one's focus. Currently, with the ever-increasing amount of technical knowledge available to inform different soccer topics, the effective use of colors as visual stimuli to enhance memory retention is crucial during the mind-mapping process. By assigning each topic a specific color this helps to:

- Grab your attention
- Make the mind map more attractive and exciting
- Improve clarity
- Make the different topics easily distinguishable
- Enhance the brain's ability to form rational time-saving methods by connecting the branches and extended details within each topic

TOP TIP

When using color for topics in your mind maps, be aware of the message you are trying to convey. Too many colors can become visually overwhelming and therefore be counterproductive.

In the mind-mapping examples, green is used for the Attacking topic which can be linked to the green light for "go" and red is used for the Defending topic which can be linked to the red light for "stop." This is advantageous to the coach as the addition of colors supports the brain's nature to link ideas and form associations. In simple terms, green can represent moving forward (e.g., being on the offensive in a soccer game) and red can represent coming to a stop or stopping (e.g., stopping goals being conceded).

Images

In addition to using color, the use of images enhances the remembering of different sub-topics. Similar to the use of colors, images must be relevant to the concept it is linked to for maximum cognitive impact. For example, using an image of a scale for the concept of balance within the concept of defensive principles of play forms a mental connection and helps the coach remember this technical knowledge.

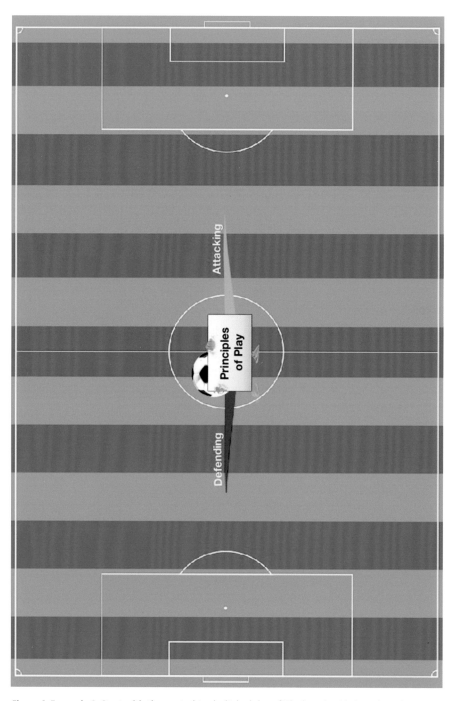

Figure 1 Example 1: Start with the central topic (Principles of Play) and add the sub-topics (Defending and Attacking) in different colors (red and green).

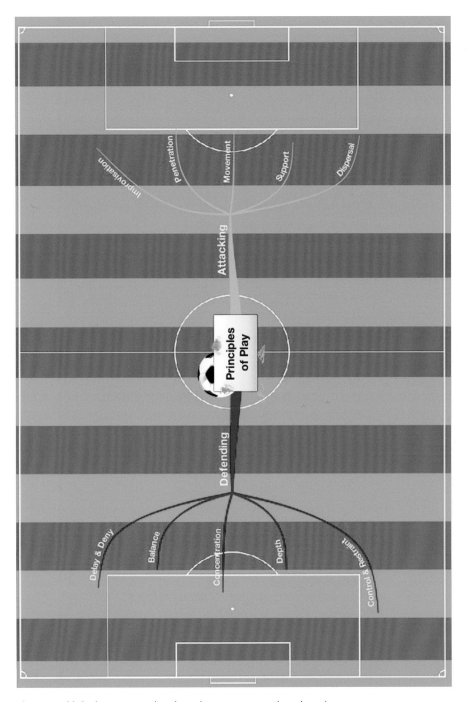

Figure 2 Add the key concepts in a branch structure onto the sub-topics.

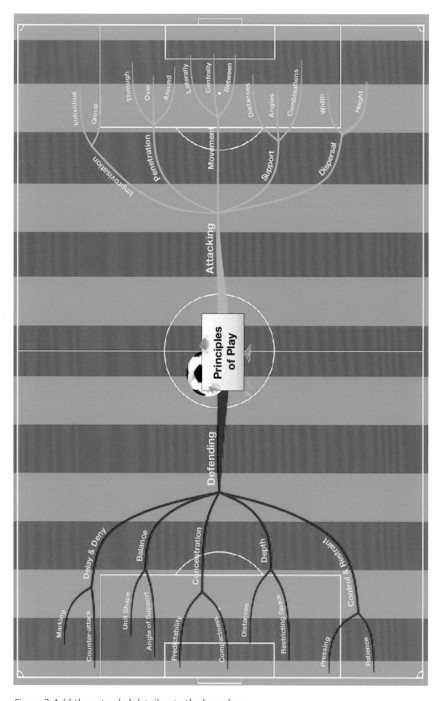

Figure 3 Add the extended detail onto the branches.

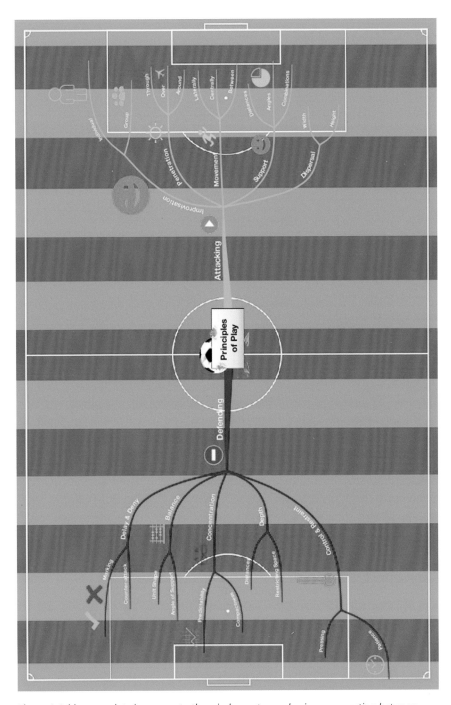

Figure 4 Add appropriate images onto the mind map to emphasize a connection between certain words.

Deconstructing a Topic

The mind-mapping technique can also be used to identify coaching points within a specific topic. A key aspect to developing coach expertise involves the ability to plan effectively. Before outlining the coaching points to be covered, it is essential to ask yourself the key questions that will help you identify the main points you intend to deliver:

- What are the details within the topic to be covered?

- What is achievable for your group of players by the end of the session?

- What are the desired learning outcomes of the session?

- How familiar are the players with this topic?

- What is the playing experience level of the players (e.g., elite, grassroots)?

- What are the players' understanding of the topic (establishing a baseline)?

- Are the coaching points both relevant and realistic within the time frame you have to work with the players?

- Is the topic being explored over an extended period of time (this would enable a slower flow of information)?

Within the mind map (example 2a) there will be both central and peripheral coaching points, which can be explored throughout the session. The central coaching points are those which are necessary for the topic outcomes to be achieved, whereas the peripheral coaching points facilitate progression of the session.

It is also essential that your coaching points follow a logical order to ensure that there is a clear journey through the topic. For instance, from the "Playing Out From the Back" mind map, the session focus could start with the goalkeeper before progressing to the defenders, midfielders, and finally the striker (playing out from the back).

Deconstructing a Skill

Similarly to deconstructing a topic, the mind-mapping technique can be used to support your understanding of an isolated technique or skill. In order for the individual player to perform the desired action appropriately a coach must know what the necessary building blocks are. The mind map in example 3a provides a general overview of the different aspects to consider within the technique of finishing.

Understanding the Context

While we appreciate that the mind maps in examples 2a and 3a provide a generic overview of a specific topic and isolated technique, the coaching context for each individual is undoubtedly distinctive. The depth of coaching information for an 8-year-old player will be vastly different from that required for a 21-year-old player. Likewise, the coaching expectations vary between grassroots through to the elite level and considerations for factors such as the time of year or the arrival of new players will also have a telling impact. For instance, you might have a new player who is accustomed to playing long passes from a fullback position, but your club's philosophy may be for fullbacks to play shorter passes through midfield. As a result, additional emphasis and time will most likely have to be spent on focusing on this aspect of playing out from the back, which means you will be required to go into greater depth on your mind map to know and understand the roles and responsibilities for the fullback. On the other hand, you could have a player returning from a knee injury and you are working on isolated passing techniques. Therefore, you could choose specifically to highlight the requirements of the standing foot and of the striking foot to ensure that the technique is being properly performed. Now compare examples 2b and 3b, and identify changes to the mind map depending on the context.

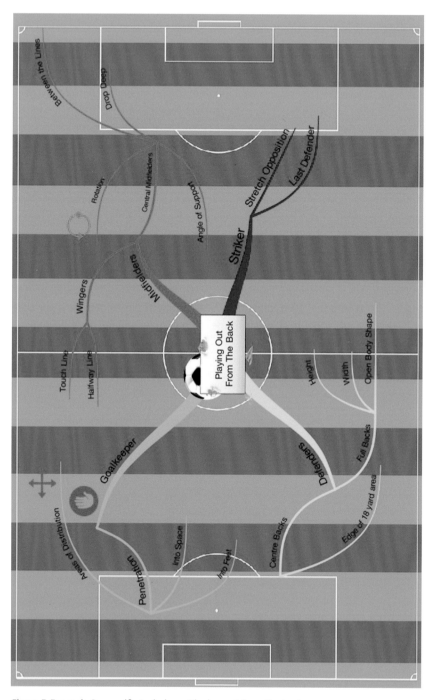

Figure 5 Example 2a specific technique: Playing out from the back

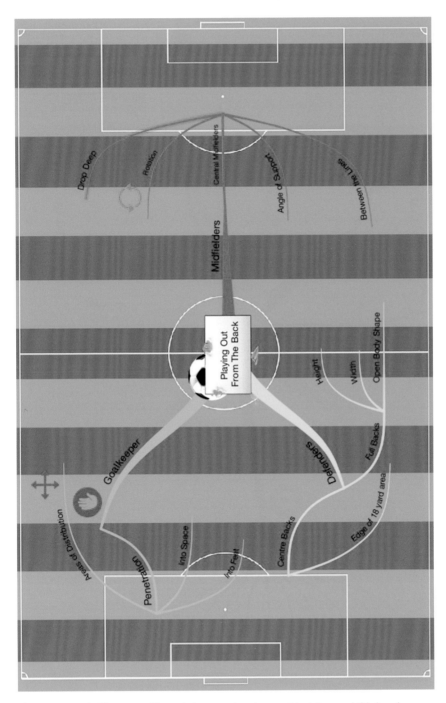

Figure 6 Example 2b context: You only have twelve players at training, and this is only the second time you will be covering the topic.

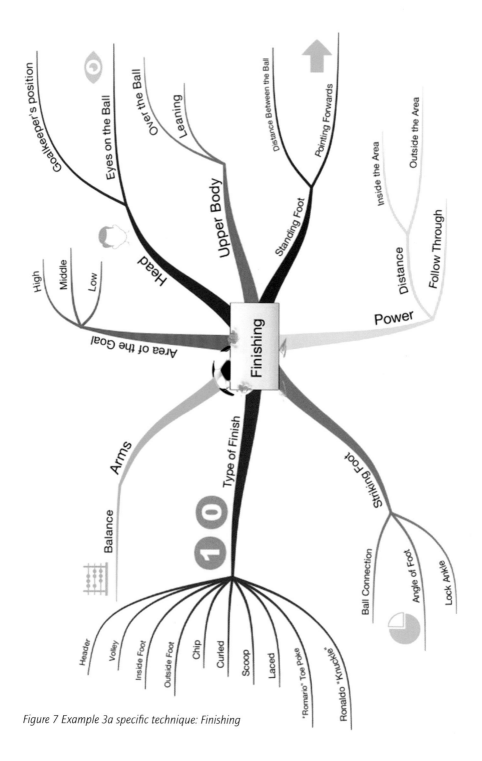

Figure 7 Example 3a specific technique: Finishing

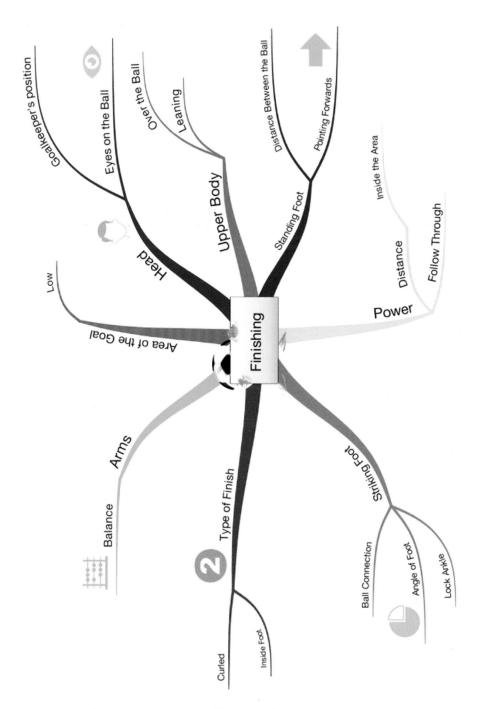

Figure 8 Example 3b context: You are coaching a U10 player who has been at your club for two months, but has been playing soccer since U7.

EXERCISE 1

Now it's time to try your own.

1. Select your themes. There are examples following of general, specific, or technical- and skill-related themes that you can choose from.
2. Use the following pages with blank soccer pitches and player silhouettes to draw a few mind maps.

TOP TIP

Consider the background to be used for your mind map. Traditionally a neutral white background is used, but you can use a relevant background to emphasize a particular topic (e.g., using a background of the 18-yard area to emphasize a finishing topic).

Sample Themes

General

- Principles of play
- Attacking
- Defending
- Transition
- Counterattacking

Technical- and Skill-Related

- Passing techniques
- Crossing techniques
- Finishing techniques
- 1-v-1 defending
- Defensive headers

Specific

- Compactness in midfield
- Defending in wide areas
- Playing out from the back
- Playing through the thirds
- Attacking quickly after regaining possession in the attacking third

But before you start consider this...

Keep Up to Date

To maximize the use of the mind-mapping learning tool and support your development of expert behaviors, it's essential to research and record new information to keep up to date. With the vast array of information now readily available at a click of a button, the retrieval of coaching knowledge is both a quicker and easier process. But also remember that your colleagues, peers, mentors, and tutors are also great sources of information.

So go ahead.

Ready, steady, mind map!

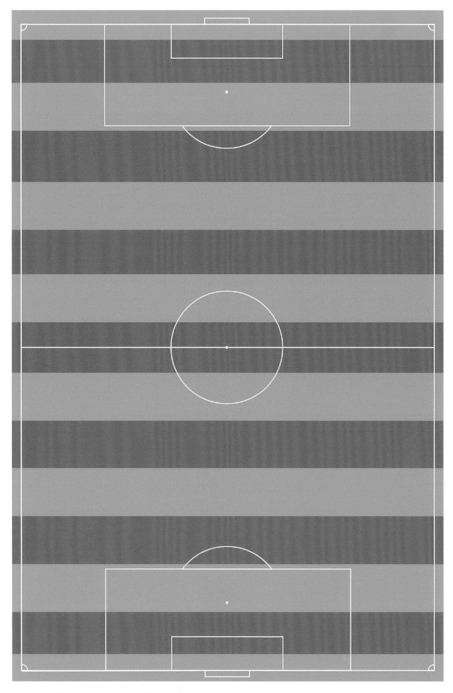

Figure 9 Mind maps: General theme (1)

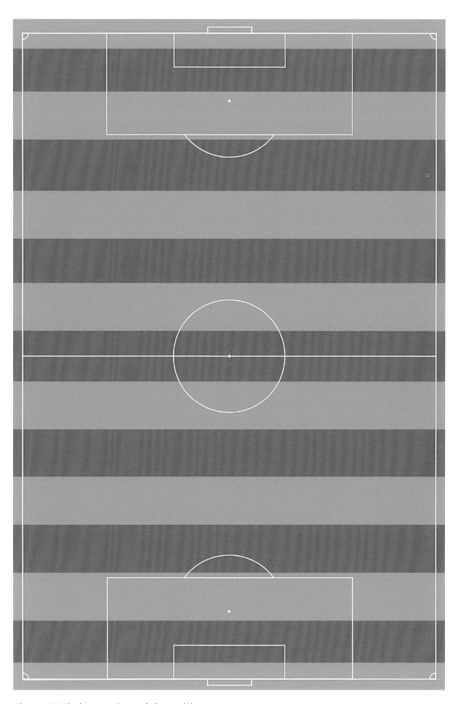

Figure 10 Mind maps: General theme (2)

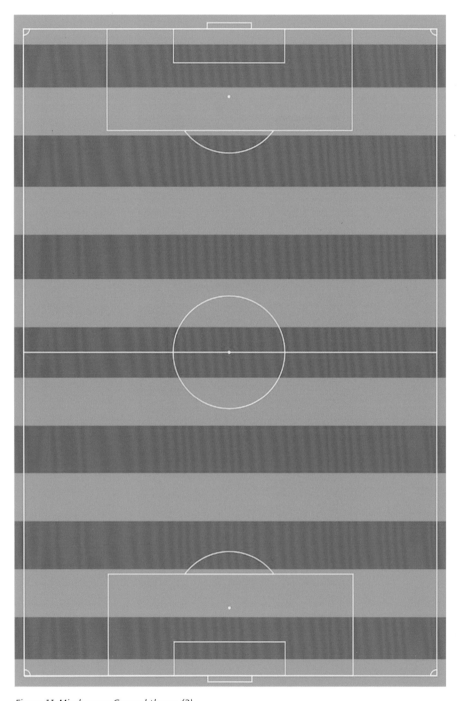

Figure 11 Mind maps: General theme (3)

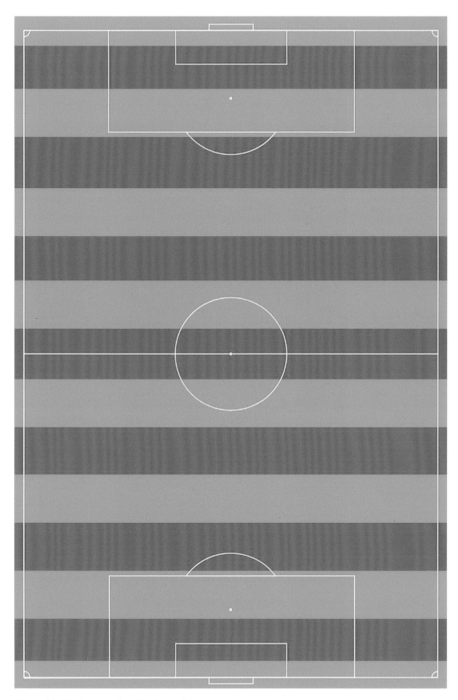

Figure 12 Mind maps: Specific theme (1)

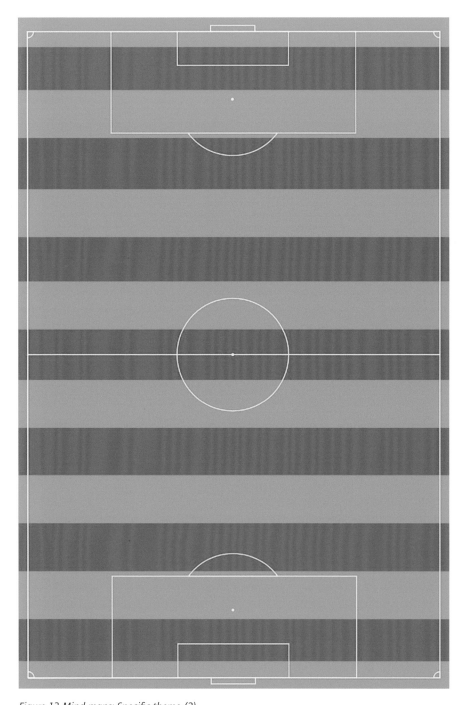

Figure 13 Mind maps: Specific theme (2)

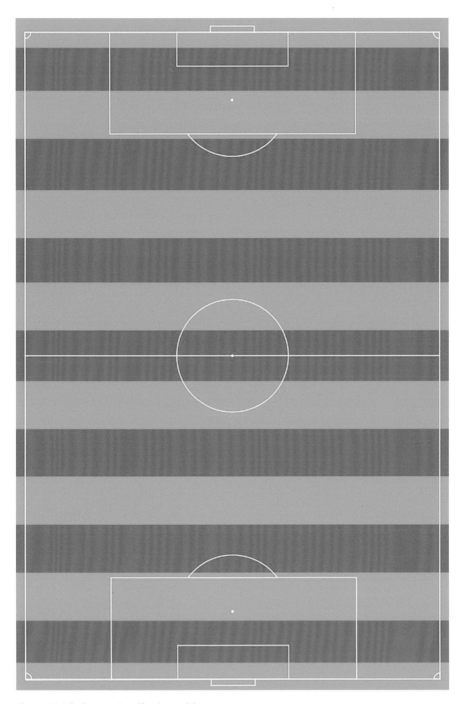

Figure 14 Mind maps: Specific theme (3)

Figure 15 Mind maps: Technical- and skill-related theme (1)

Figure 16 Mind maps: Technical- and skill-related theme (2)

Figure 17 Mind maps: Technical- and skill-related theme (3)

The Mind-Mapping Speed Test

Not only is the ability to recall information critical, the speed of the recollection is just as important. From the moment a coach says "Stop," "Pause," "Relax," or "Rewind," the coaching points delivered must be clear, concise, and, most importantly, relevant to the reason for stopping the practice in the first place.

With this mind-mapping speed test you will be able to see how much information you recall about a general theme, topic, or technique within a given amount of time. After choosing a theme, give yourself two minutes to recall as much information as you can in relation to that theme. This is important, as you want to try and generate a sense of urgency to replicate how you would deliver coaching points under a constrained period of time in training sessions. Following your first attempt, reduce your time by 20 seconds each day and repeat with the same theme. Leave at least a day between each attempt and at the end of the week you will be able to analyze your personal performance. In example 4 we have used a heading theme to demonstrate what the process could look like.

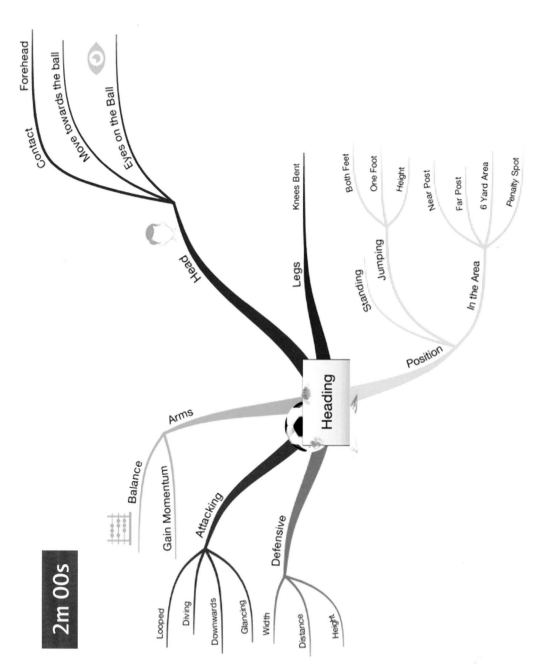

Figure 18 Mind-mapping speed test: First attempt

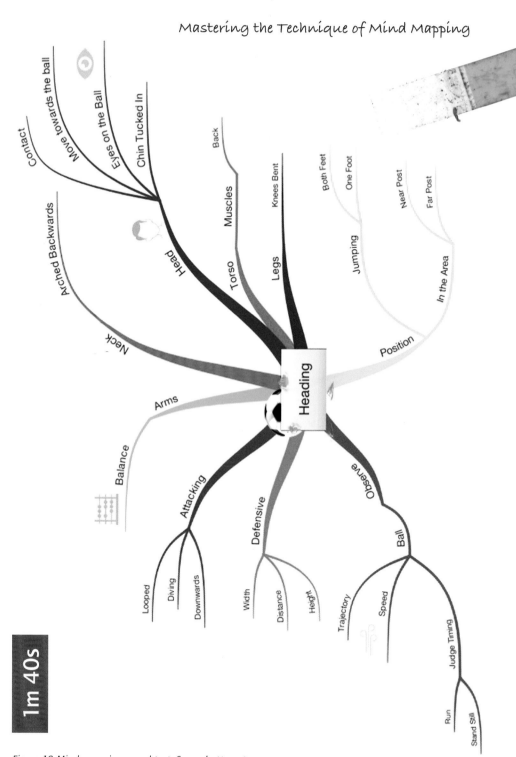

Figure 19 Mind-mapping speed test: Second attempt

1m 40s

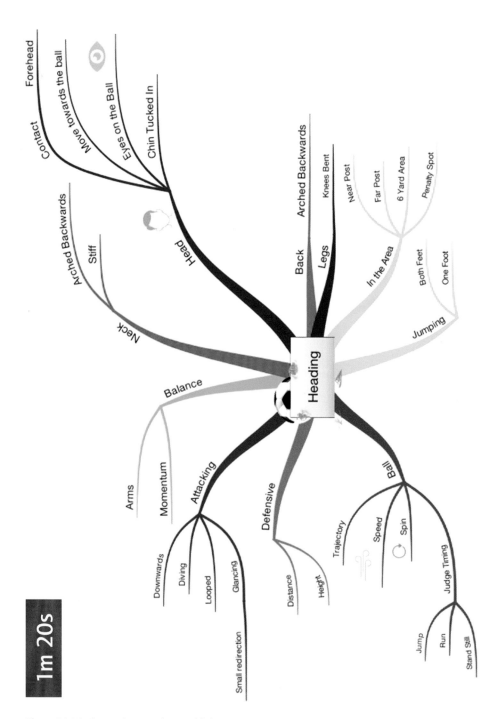

Figure 20 Mind-mapping speed test: Third attempt

1m 20s

Speed Test Analysis

In the example provided you will notice a difference between each mind map, such as the amount of information, number of branches, number of images, and so on. That is why it's important to ask yourself the following questions:

- What did I notice?
- Which pieces of information did I consistently remember?
- Which pieces of information did I always group together?
- Which images did I use to help me remember?
- How does my information relate to the central topic?

After this generic overview it would also be helpful to have a quantitative element to your analysis. Table 2 shows a simple and effective method to achieve this.

Table 2 Example of mind-mapping speed test analysis: Heading

Word or phrase	Number of times remembered	Position	Image
Arched backwards	3	Branch (x3)	
Arms	3	Sub-topic (x2) Branch	
Attacking	3	Sub-topic (x3)	
Back	2	Sub-topic Sub-branch	
Balance	3	Sub-topic Branch (x2)	2
Ball	2	Sub-topic Branch	
Both feet	3	Branch (x2) Sub-branch	
Chin tucked in	2	Branch (x2)	
Contact	3	Branch (x3)	
Defensive	3	Sub-topic	
Distance	3	Branch (x3)	
Diving	3	Branch (x3)	
Downward	3	Branch (x3)	
Eyes on the ball	3	Branch (x3)	3
Far post	3	Branch Sub-branch (x2)	
Forehead	2	Sub-branch (x2)	

Word or phrase	Number of times remembered	Position	Image
Gain momentum	1	Branch	
Glancing	2	Branch (x2)	
Head	3	Sub-topic	3
Height	4	Branch (x3) Sub-branch	
In the area	3	Sub-topic Branch (x2)	
Jumping	3	Sub-topic Branch (x2)	
Jump	1	Sub-branch	
Judge timing	2	Branch Sub-branch	
Knees bent	3	Branch (x3)	
Legs	3	Sub-topic (x3)	
Looped	3	Branch (x3)	
Move toward the ball	3	Branch (x3)	
Momentum	1	Branch	
Muscles	1	Branch	
Near post	3	Branch Sub-branch (x2)	
Neck	2	Sub-topic	
Observe	1	Sub-topic	

(continued)

Table 2 (continued)

Word or phrase	Number of times remembered	Position	Image
One foot	3	Branch Sub-branch (x2)	
Penalty spot	2	Branch Sub-branch	
Position	2	Sub-topic (x2)	
Run	2	Sub-branch (x2)	
Small redirection	1	Sub-branch	
Speed	2	Branch Sub-branch	2
Spin	1	Branch	1
Standing	1	Branch	
Stand still	2	Sub-branch (x2)	
Stiff	1	Branch	
Torso	1	Sub-topic	
Trajectory	2	Branch Sub-branch	
Width	2	Branch (x2)	
Six-yard area	2	Branch Sub-branch	

You might be thinking something along the lines of "That's a lot of information." Don't worry. Your brain holds so much information it can often be surprising when you put numbers and figures to it! So let's take a closer look at what this all means.

- A total of 46 different words or phrases were remembered across the three mind maps

- The word height was remembered the most amount of times with a score of 4

- 21 words or phrases were remembered three times

- 15 words or phrases were remembered twice

- 10 words or phrases were remembered once

- 11 words or phrases were remembered in the same position on three occasions

- 5 words or phrases had an image attached to them

As a coach, one can be confident that those words and phrases recalled the most amount of times are easier to retrieve from memory. Research has shown that this is because the nerve pathways formed by the brain when encoding (creating a brand new memory) have been revisited a greater number of times, thereby strengthening these pathways which allows for quicker memory recall. On the flip side, the nerve pathways for words and phrases remembered the least amount of times needs to be revisited more often. One way of achieving this could be to link purposefully an image to those words and phrases remembered once.

How Do I Know What I Know?

Sound familiar? Well, like millions of other coaches this is a frequently asked personal question. Ultimately this speed test will provide you with an indication of and tangible evidence into how your brain remembers and connects different pieces of information. The patterns you identify can help you to clearly recognize your strengths and weaknesses in memory recall.

Use the mind maps on the following three pages to test your ability to recall information within a specific technique, topic, or theme. Record your results and pay attention to what you noticed.

2m 00s

Figure 21 Mind map: Sample 1

1m 40s

Figure 22 Mind map: Sample 2

1m 20s

Figure 23 Mind map: Sample 3

Remember to think through these questions as you are completing your speed test analysis table:

- What did I notice?
- Which pieces of information did I consistently remember?
- Which pieces of information did I always group together?
- Which images did I use to help me remember?
- How does my information relate to the central topic?

Table 3 Mind-mapping speed test Analysis

Word or phrase	Number of times remembered	Position	Image

Word or phrase	Number of times remembered	Position	Image

Word or phrase	Number of times remembered	Position	Image

Record your thoughts here:

1.3 TIME FOR A RECAP

In this chapter you have learned:

1. The science behind mind mapping and how your brain works
2. How to construct a mind map for general, specific, and technique- or skill-related themes
3. To consider the context you are working in when creating a mind map
4. How to use the mind-mapping speed test to analyze your ability to recall different pieces of information

Remember:

✔ You are in control of the process and your learning.
✔ Be creative! They're your mind maps so make sure they make sense to you.
✔ Create. Pause. Reflect.

1.4 WHAT TO EXPECT NEXT

The next chapter focuses on how you can develop the key characteristics of an expert coach. Mind maps will be used to help you identify your current level, while the concept of intentionally participating in purposeful practice will help you on your journey.

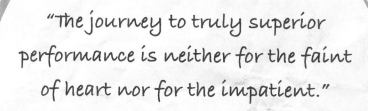

"The journey to truly superior performance is neither for the faint of heart nor for the impatient."

Ericsson, Prietula, & Cokley, 2007

 **DEVELOPING EXPERTISE**

2.1 THE SCIENCE OF COACHING

The modern-day coach is expected to deliver a high level of professional expertise. Professional coaching is now on a par with teaching and other educational professions. There is however a significant difference in that coaches are judged on the performance of their athletes. This can often be quite arbitrary as a coach has no direct control over the players that they will be working with. Moreover the skills of the professional coach are now rapidly expanding to off-the-pitch activities such as doing performance reviews, writing feedback, and liaising effectively with support staff (e.g., physiotherapists, sport scientists, video analysts, and psychologists). Often these aspects of the professional coach are learned on the job with varying degrees of success.

Until recently, coaching has only been loosely described as an art. Indeed, no longer has the notion of instinct alone been accepted as a blanket explanation for the effectiveness of the expert coach. Importantly, psychological research has shown that self-awareness plays a pivotal role in personal development, which the coaching arena can certainly benefit from. In soccer it is commonplace for many ex-professional players who have progressed quickly through their qualifications to assume that they are more or less fully equipped to be a high-performing coach. Although a level of playing expertise might be present, the truth is that they are probably only expert in one area and a comparative novice in creating an effective learning environment for their players.

This can be highly problematic, as coaches may genuinely believe that they have certain skills already. For example, an Under-18s coach might assume that they are an expert coach and overestimate their ability to coach at an expert level from U8s and upward. Similarly, an experienced professional might believe, and wrongly assume, that due to their experience of working with and observing top coaches in their career that they are now able to replicate similar behaviors with the same outcomes.

In light of these conclusions, it is reasonable to suggest that coaches who exhibit a lack of self-awareness have an unrealistic understanding of the qualities needed to develop through the stages of an expert coach. Hence, the understanding of one's coaching competencies and behaviors, through effective self-assessment, appears to be an essential step in bridging the gap.

The Science of Expertise

Recently there has been a growing body of scientific knowledge originated by Anders Ericsson in his extensive research into what he calls the science of expertise. Through his research he has identified some very important and useful ways that idea can be applied to anyone who wants to become an expert. The following section explores some of the important concepts and ideas, and suggests ways that you can adopt this method of practice to help you foster an excellentist approach to your coaching. This approach embraces the striving for excellence as opposed to wanting to be perfect.

We know that experts do things differently from novices. They solve problems differently; they have enhanced perception as well as extensive and specialised knowledge. They have the ability to reflect effectively and quickly identify what needs to be done. What is clear is that expert coaches are not simply competent coaches with more experience. They fundamentally do things differently. This is true for all experts across all domains, and is applicable within coaching.

Dreyfus's Skill–Acquisition Model

The philosopher Hubert Dreyfus (1986) developed the five-stage model of skill acquisition which describes how adults move through different stages of practice until they reach expertise. It is a universal model that can be applied to any profession, and it is a useful starting point to consider which stage you are currently at in your coaching development.

Accepting a staged model of professional development encourages a different approach to our progression. First, learning happens in stages rather than as a straightforward linear progression from novice to expert. Second, each stage is characterised by differentiated knowledge and skills, and third, higher performance requires progression through different learning phases.

Furthermore, not everyone becomes an expert. Experts manage the challenges of coaching with intuition and creativity-this sets them apart from their less skilled colleagues.

Consider the five stages below and ask yourself questions such as: Does this describe me? Do I do this? Be honest with yourself when making this judgement.

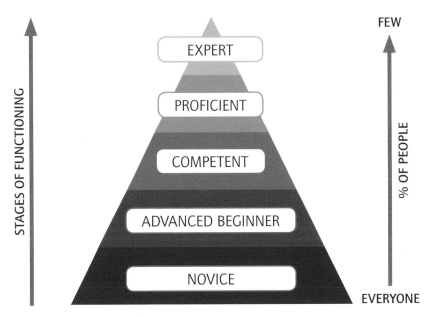

Figure 24 Five stages of the skill–acquisition model

Stage 1: Novice

Novices are beginners. They need considerable guidance to accomplish tasks and are very reliant on using previously learned rules to determine their actions. They often do not recognize that the situation demands something different. They will not feel responsible for anything other than following the rules. Sometimes this knowledge is referred to as textbook knowledge, which is very rigid.

In order for novices to improve, they need close monitoring and supervision, which provides them with the guidance that they need. Novices generally have lower self-confidence and require positive feedback to help them persevere. (From a coaching perspective this may well be only following a session plan that they have learned.) They may be able to replicate something, but they will be unable to recognize such things as the different needs of the players, or to modify the session because players are tired.

Stage 2: Advanced Beginner

The advanced beginner has had some experience of the real world's demands and is starting to develop coping strategies to help solve problems. They use the rules that they have learned, but also begin to understand that different situational factors are important in determining their actions. Through their increased experiences they are beginning to recognize when situations are similar, how they should respond, and when situations are different. It is still difficult for them to change an action once they have begun it though, so for example if they are putting on a session that they had done before but with a different group of players, it is difficult for them to appreciate that the session might need to be modified to meet the differing needs of the players. Guidance is still needed to highlight and eliminate mistakes in their practice. However, confidence will begin to grow as they accrue more hours of practice. The more real world experience that they gain the better able they are to understand how to adapt their practice.

Stage 3: Competence

At this stage coaches are now able to organise the rules into more complex conceptual models that are more flexible and work well in a range of situations. Moreover, they are now willing to accept responsibility for their decisions. They are beginning to be able to understand the bigger picture, and how elements fit together. They still need practice and it is important that this is in a range of different coaching situations (e.g., a U10s boys' group, a mixed-ability recreational session, or a more experienced U18s girls' squad). This enables coaches to understand how they need to apply key principles and concepts while at the same time recognizing that they need to adapt to meet the differing needs of the players they are working with.

However, they are now able to begin to set goals and start to develop some long-term planning around their own development. They are also able to use contingency planning, so for example if they had planned a session for twelve players but only ten turn up to train, they will have begun to think about what they should do in this situation and have a plan B at the ready. They now have higher self-confidence in their abilities and need less direct guidance. However, in order to progress they still need feedback and support from someone with expertise.

Stage 4: Proficient

This stage is demonstrated by competency, underpinned by knowledge and understanding of the discipline. Performance is fundamentally based on their experience and they are also able to work independently on most tasks. They have accrued many thousands of hours of practice across different contexts which will have necessitated that they adapt and change their actions accordingly. They are able to give guidance to novices and advanced beginners on how to perform the basics and routine elements of the skills. However, if a task is outside the normal practices, they still need guidance and supervision.

Moreover they are able to have a holistic understanding of the role rather than seeing it as separate parts. This impacts their ability to make rational choices because they consider fewer aspects to arrive at their decision thereby speeding up the process. They are also able to recognize when there is deviation from the expected and put into place appropriate actions. They are able to use others' experiences and knowledge to enhance their own practice.

Many coaches never move beyond this stage, although they might be fooled into thinking that simply because they have been coaching for a long time they are experts. Another trap that soccer coaches fall into is assuming that the age of the player the coach is working with reflects the competency of the coach. Thus the coach working with the U18s is assumed to be more expert than the coach working with the U10s.

Stage 5: Expertise

The key hallmark of an expert is that they simply do what works. They often work intuitively because they are able to recognize quickly a situation and know what is needed, seemingly effortlessly. This is because they have acquired an enormous amount of content knowledge, which they organize in ways that reflect a deep understanding. Because of this they are able to apply quickly the right solution at the right time. This is the coach who is able to jump into a session and make small adjustments that seem to change the outcome. They are always responsive to individual player needs and create sessions that ensure each player has their needs met from the session.

So not only do they have a vast library they also have an excellent retrieval system. Even though they are so skilled an expert might not be able to articulate exactly how they do things. This is often played out in soccer where brilliant players are hired as coaches only to fail because they struggle to articulate how they solved the problem. Often the best coaches were not the best players.

Although this seems to be the final stage, an important characteristic of experts is that they never stand still. They are constantly continuing to challenge and develop themselves; everyone else is playing catch-up. Innovation is often a feature of expert practitioners, and they are likely to be practicing in ways that are ahead of their time. These are the people who create new knowledge and practices, and they are able to teach others how to do it. Their learning is often unique and personal to them as is the way that they solve problems. They will deliberately seek out ways to improve their learning in both formal and informal settings. Sometimes because of this perceived difference they are not always understood, and the newness of their approach can be difficult for others to accept.

In coaching, research has identified some critical factors that define the characteristics of expert coaches. Indeed, Wiman and his colleagues (2010) identified these personal aspects of coaches to separate the expert from the merely competent. They found that experts demonstrate dedication and commitment to coaching which underlies all that they do and which creates a drive and a passion to keep on developing. Furthermore, expert coaches have an open-mindedness for change whether that be of self, others, technique, or coaching methods. This is demonstrated by a willingness to learn and to keep learning. Engaging in active knowledge acquisition (i.e., constantly looking for learning opportunities that will enhance your practice) is another factor that separates experts from others. The drive to be constantly improving through a variety of methods is a critical factor that defines the expert. These different methods have been defined as mediated learning which is formal learning such as taught courses and conferences; unmediated learning which is self-driven learning through seeking out mentors or other experts who can help you develop; and internal learning through self-reflection and self-analysis.

Part of this openness is the acceptance of criticism, the ability to listen to others, and an acknowledgement that they may need help in areas of weakness. These personal characteristics enable expert coaches to establish positive relationships with their athletes.

Application of the Dreyfus Model

So what can be learned from this model? First, it is important that you honestly acknowledge what stage of the model you are actually at. This will help you understand how you are currently practicing. Second, it has been found that when you are working on developing your expertise, it is most effective to find a mentor who is no more than two stages above you. This will optimize your development and learning. As you become more proficient, you will need to change your mentors. Lastly, it is important that you ensure that you are learning in a way that is appropriate to where you currently are. This is also important if you are responsible for the development and learning of others.

We have created a generalized mind map which identifies the key characteristics and core skills of an expert coach. Take some time to consider this in relation to your current practice and self-assess each of the characteristics from 1 to 5 where 1 = novice, 2 = advanced beginner, 3 = competent, 4 = proficient, and 5 = expert. Then use the second mind map to make your numerical additions to get a general overview of where you think you currently are in each characteristic.

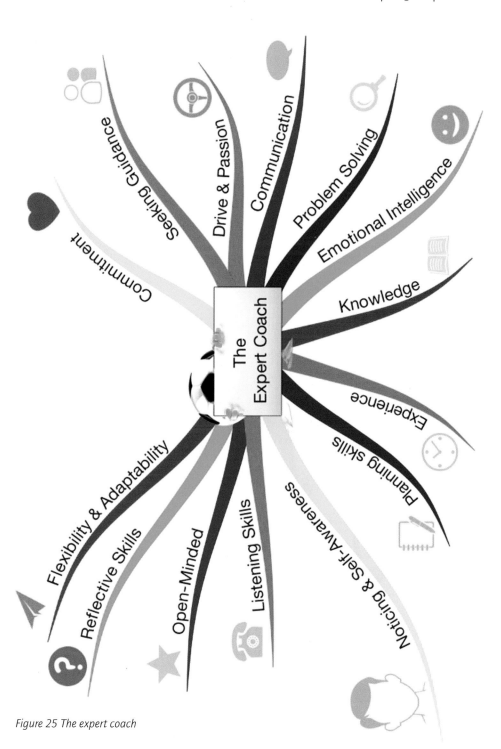

Figure 25 The expert coach

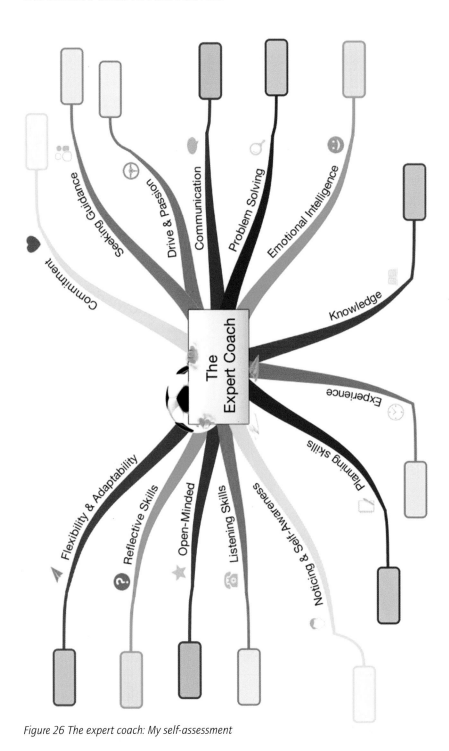

Figure 26 The expert coach: My self-assessment

Following your self-assessment think about each characteristic in more detail using the template below:

Characteristic:	Planning skills
Currently I am a...	3
Because...	I am confident that I can plan a session for each training practice, but I find it challenging to plan a syllabus for the entire season which links the individual sessions together.

Characteristic:	Commitment
Currently I am a...	
Because...	

Characteristic:	Communication
Currently I am a...	
Because...	

Characteristic:	Drive and passion
Currently I am a...	
Because...	

Characteristic:	Emotional intelligence
Currently I am a...	
Because...	

Characteristic:	Experience
Currently I am a...	
Because...	

Characteristic:	Flexibility and adaptability
Currently I am a...	
Because...	

Characteristic:	Knowledge
Currently I am a...	
Because...	

Characteristic:	Listening skills
Currently I am a...	
Because...	

Characteristic:	Noticing and self-awareness
Currently I am a...	
Because...	

Characteristic:	Open-mindedness
Currently I am a...	
Because...	

Characteristic:	Planning skills
Currently I am a...	
Because...	

Characteristic:	Problem solving
Currently I am a...	
Because...	

Characteristic:	Reflective skills
Currently I am a...	
Because...	

Characteristic:	Seeking guidance
Currently I am a...	
Because...	

Who Are the Experts That You Can Learn From?

This is a question of considering who has relevant expertise that you can learn from. For example, if you want to develop your expertise in working with young players, it might be appropriate to observe school teachers of the same age group as they are likely to be experts at a range of key skills that you need (e.g., class management, teaching a mixed-ability class, and communication skills). Or maybe you need to develop expertise in planning and organization. Can you identify someone who does that at an expert level? The point here is that your experts might not simply come from within soccer, so by considering the actual skills you want to develop objectively, your method of developing your skills becomes much more focused.

Once you have identified who the expert is that you want to learn from try to understand what they do that makes them successful. You will of course have to consider exactly what success looks like. This is easy if you are considering soccer players—they are the ones playing in the Premier League or in the World Cup—but it is harder when you are identifying the expert coaches. Often these experts are less visible, especially if you are looking for the experts who work within the developmental phase of soccer. Furthermore, finding a means to assess their performances objectively can also be difficult. However, it is important that you do this and that you identify what exactly separates these coaches from others and what training methods have gotten them there.

SKILL	EXPERT
Stretching	• Gymnastics coach • Strength and conditioning coach
Communication with U9s	• Primary school teacher • Current U9s coach
Player Reviews	• Head coach • Teacher

Figure 27 Example skill experts

Can you identify some skills that you want to develop and who the expert might be to help you? If you can't identify someone that you know who has the relevant expertise, use your network to help you.

Now complete this table to focus your attention on what areas you specifically want to develop and who can help you.

SKILL	EXPERT

Figure 28 Identify the skills you wish to develop and the possible experts who might help.

2.2 HOW TO PRACTICE WITH PURPOSE

Purposeful practice has been highlighted by Anders Ericsson and Robert Pool (2016) as the most important factor in developing expertise. In their book they discuss in detail the misconception of the label talented. This label is often put on individuals in sport, which seems to suggest that elite athlete's achievements somehow come naturally. But what you actually find is that people who have been called talented have been practicing purposefully for many years. It is this that separates them, not some innate ability. No one is born with the ability to play or coach soccer. Successful people have been engaging with their professional practice and development in a purposeful way for many years. The critical message from Ericsson and Pool is that if we all practice purposefully we have the potential to become experts.

There are a number of key elements to purposeful practice. These need to become second nature if you are to become an expert. Purposeful practice challenges you to leave your comfort zone, to try to do something that you couldn't do before. It is only by constantly pushing your personal boundaries that you will be able to move towards expertise. Sometimes the most difficult transition is when you are already proficient. The easy option is to stop at proficiency because you will be able to function effectively most of the time. In order to rise above this level, you have to accept and be open to both make mistakes and learn from those mistakes. Moving out of your comfort zone means that you will make mistakes and things won't always work well. This can be difficult and often requires a different mind-set. It is a learning process and you are not an expert...YET. This is especially important for novice coaches as it can be very frustrating when your training sessions don't go as you want them to. It is at this point that you have to acknowledge where you are on the expertise ladder and manage and adjust your expectations accordingly.

Applying the principles below will enable you to become purposeful:

1. Have clear goals and intentions.
2. Ensure you stay focused and present when you are coaching. Notice the detail.
3. Use feedback effectively to notice what needs to change.
4. Solve the problems and find a solution.

These principles can be summarized by the 3F principle:

FOCUS ▸ FEEDBACK ▸ FIX-IT

Finding Your Focus

This book endeavors to help you with all aspects of purposeful practice and shows you effective tools that will enhance your development. Let's start with how you create a focus for your practice. In order to identify your focus, you first need to consider what area you think you need to work on and improve. Using the mind-mapping technique can help you to self-assess and to identify the key elements that contribute to your professional practice. The sample mind map used highlights the communication characteristic of an expert coach as the specific focus.

Now draw your own mind map and go into detail for one of the expert coach characteristics you want to focus on over the next two weeks.

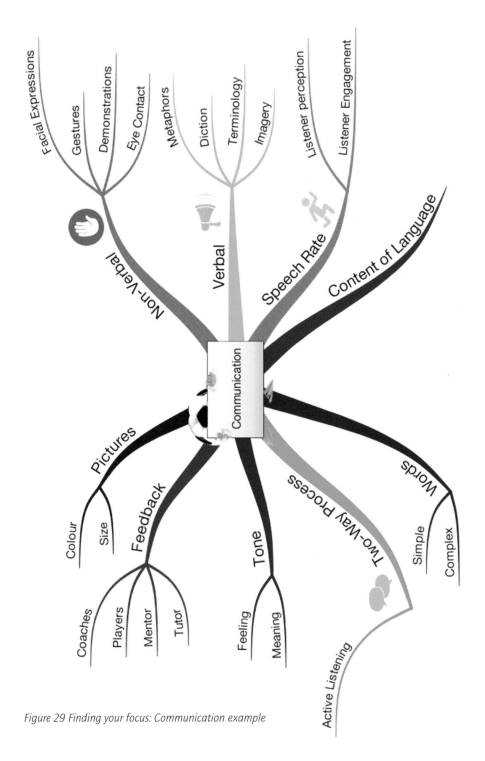

Figure 29 Finding your focus: Communication example

From the mind map you can now begin to set your intentions or goals. This process is important because this gives you the FOCUS for next the session. However, it is important which type of intentions you set. Below is a diagram that highlights the different types of intentions that you can set for yourself. Consider each of them in turn and then decide which you think is the most effective.

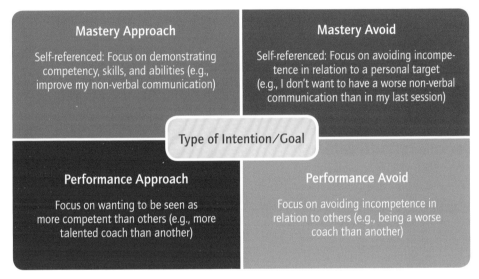

Mastery Approach

Self-referenced: Focus on demonstrating competency, skills, and abilities (e.g., improve my non-verbal communication)

Mastery Avoid

Self-referenced: Focus on avoiding incompetence in relation to a personal target (e.g., I don't want to have a worse non-verbal communication than in my last session)

Type of Intention/Goal

Performance Approach

Focus on wanting to be seen as more competent than others (e.g., more talented coach than another)

Performance Avoid

Focus on avoiding incompetence in relation to others (e.g., being a worse coach than another)

Figure 30 Different intentions or goals diagram

The answer is the mastery approach. This is because it is important that you set challenges that are self-referenced and not dependent upon anyone else in order for you to achieve them. Furthermore, by setting a performance approach or goals of things to avoid, you will be reliant on the performance of other people to achieve success because you do not have any control over the actions of others. Your success and failure should be entirely in your hands and controlled by your actions.

There are times when you may find it difficult to maintain your focus. Understanding how your focus can get disrupted can be helpful as it is an indicator of what your internal barriers may be. The most common type of loss of focus is being distracted (vigilance, fatigue). This is where you are not able to maintain a constant focus; your mind may wander to other things unrelated to what you are doing. Secondly, disengagement (isolation, not belonging) occurs when you feel separated from what is happening in the here and now. Third, disconnection (distorted) is when you are not able to notice consciously and recognize what is actually happening in the present so your world view becomes distorted.

Lastly disassociation (fear, apprehension, uncertainty) occurs when you want to avoid things that are currently happening. When you can't maintain your focus, it is helpful to ask yourself what type of issue it is. By doing this you will gain greater insight into yourself and understand what is potentially tripping you up and stopping you from being fully engaged.

Function of Feedback

In essence there are two main sources of feedback: internal and external. These offer us an important opportunity to check how we are doing against our goals and intentions. The internal process is generally referred to as reflection and we discuss in detail later on how you can become skilled at doing this. However asking yourself critical questions such as:

- What did I notice?
- What actions did I take?
- Why did I make that choice?
- What were my mistakes?
- When and where was I making them?
- What could I have done differently?
- Do I have the fundamental skills?

This will help you become more aware of how you are doing things; by honestly engaging in this process your aim is to become an expert error detector.

External feedback can come in a range of guises from the feedback your players give you, to other coaches around you, video feedback, mentor feedback, and formal and informal assessment feedback from coaching courses to name but a few. When you are seeking out external feedback, it is important that you do so in relation to the goal or intention that you have set yourself, otherwise the feedback can be unfocused. If there are discrepancies, this is a useful point of learning.

How to Fix It

The last stage of purposeful practice is that you use the feedback to assess which aspects need to change, and more importantly identify a process through which you will be able to achieve this. So fixing it is thinking in detail about how you are going to use the feedback to improve what you are currently doing. Coming up with a clear plan of action is essential.

Sometimes we think that if we just try harder we will be able to succeed. However this is not necessarily the solution. It may be that you need to try differently, come up with a new practice strategy, look beyond the obvious. If you're not improving it's because you aren't practicing the right way, so you need to figure out what the right way is. This is where you can engage the help of others as they might have some helpful ideas. It is important if you want to become an expert that you challenge the notion of good enough. An expert is constantly striving and wanting to be better, so if you are satisfied with good enough you may never develop beyond proficiency.

Lastly be aware of your mind-set. If you notice that you are having limiting thoughts such as "I can't," "It's too hard," "I'm not talented or good enough," these will inevitably have an impact on your confidence and belief in yourself. When we are working outside of our comfort zone, things won't always go smoothly; there will be mistakes and challenges along the way. But welcome these as this is where you have the greatest opportunity to grow and develop. By asking yourself "What did I learn from that?" or "What did that experience teach me that I needed to know?," you can think about how you will change or fix it in the future.

Now what happens after setting your intentions? What do you notice about how you practice?

2.3 TIME FOR A RECAP

In this chapter you have learned:

1. About the science of coaching and developing expertise
2. The key attributes of an expert coach
3. How to practice purposefully
4. How to apply the fix-it model

Remember

✔ Developing expertise will take time.
✔ Consider the experts you can learn from.
✔ Find your focus and work on it.

2.4 WHAT TO EXPECT NEXT

Identifying your strengths as a coach can have a significant impact on your effectiveness and developing expertise. The next chapter will help you to discover your action, character, and thinking strengths.

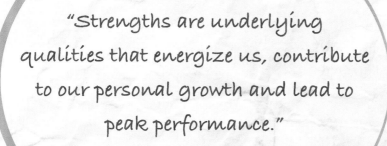

"Strengths are underlying qualities that energize us, contribute to our personal growth and lead to peak performance."

Brewerton, 2011

3 STRENGTHS-BASED LEARNING AND STRENGTHS SPOTTING

Have you ever said to your players, "Play to your strengths!" Sound familiar? How about saying the same thing to yourself as a coach? "Coach to your strengths!" This may sound—and even feel—slightly uncomfortable or awkward. If it does, it's probably because you don't actively notice and then use your strengths in a purposeful way to practice and develop as a coach. Guess what? This is not uncommon. Unsurprisingly, research presented on this topic has shown that only approximately a third of individuals actually have a significant understanding of their personal strengths (Linley, 2008). This is a missed opportunity to tap into your inner resources and maximize your individual potential. Clearly the recognition of one's strengths requires a bit of guidance and courage to be able to say "This is what I'm good at!"

Take a moment to consider carefully and think about those things you find easiest to do, or the things you feel confident that you will be successful in doing. Are a few instances coming to mind? During these moments do you feel a sense of achievement and a surge of happiness? If so, then you can safely assume that in some way you are probably using your strengths. However, some of these strengths will be more obvious than others. Fundamentally, the process of identifying, considering, and purposefully using one's strengths has its origins in positive psychology. The strengths identified extend to everyday life (e.g., being optimistic or regularly showing fairness) and are used most of the time. To help you, this section focuses on your personal attributes, specifically highlighting your strengths and qualities as a coach.

In general, the expert coach is more aware of their strengths and how best to use them to maximize their impact and effectiveness. When an individual is intentionally using their strengths, it will be easier for them to be engaged in their work and perform to a higher level for longer periods of time and with greater personal contentment. Research has shown that this strengths-based learning is informed by five key principles (Wade, 2016):

- Using our strength is the smallest action one can take to elicit the largest difference.
- Each person's character strengths are inherent.
- When maximizing our strengths, we can succeed in altering our weaknesses.
- Within the areas of our character, strengths lie in our areas of greatest potential.
- The strengths-based approach focuses primarily on that which is strong, correct, and working successfully.

Unfortunately, many people find this strengths-based approach a challenging task for a number of reasons, including a lack of self-awareness and spending more time searching for weaknesses instead of strengths. The tendency of people in general is to ruminate over personal weaknesses and shortcomings. Therefore the ability to identify one's strengths doesn't happen without intention.

3.1 TYPES OF STRENGTHS

When identifying one's strengths this can be divided into three different types: action strengths, character strengths, and thinking strengths. Each type focuses on a different element of human functioning:

- Action strengths are what you do and how you do it, and can be identified through your interaction with tasks and activities.
- Character strengths are who you are and where your inner resources lie.
- Thinking strengths are how you make sense of the world around you through your perception and understanding.

Each type is uniquely different and will reveal a wide variety of strengths you might not have been previously aware of. For example, one of your action strengths could be that you are very skilled at demonstrating different passing techniques or that you can draw pictures and images with amazing clarity. An example of a character strength could be that you know how to show gratitude to others and to show appreciation for what they have done for you. Another example of a thinking strength might be that you create mental mnemonics to remember information.

Unfortunately, as mentioned earlier, due to a considerable tendency to focus on what one is not doing well, many of us go through life without ever identifying our principal strengths, let alone using them to their full potential. Therefore, to help you on your journey of discovery, the diagram below highlights the key questions that you should consider within each strength type.

Take time to reflect, remember, and begin to be more conscious of what, how, and why you do what you do each day to help you have a clearer indication of what your strengths might be. Use the following diagram to consider your different strengths.

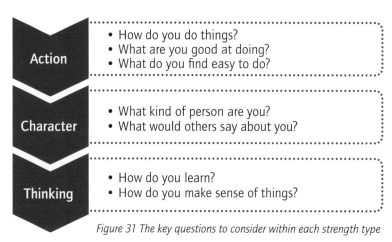

Figure 31 The key questions to consider within each strength type

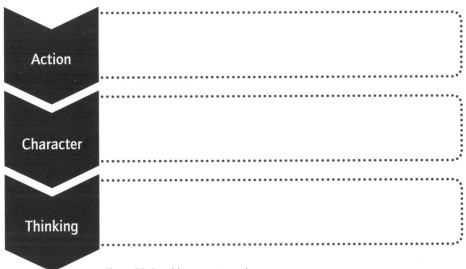

Figure 32 Consider your strengths

What did you find easy to identify? What did you find difficult? Generally people struggle to do this without guidance. The next section is designed to help you develop your ability to spot strengths.

3.2 STRENGTHS-SPOTTING EXERCISES

This section will help you identify your top five strengths within these three strengths types and put this into your own personal strengths mind map. This will enable you to keep referring back to an outline of those things you are good at and for you to remember and call upon when required. These strengths will also be used to help you strengthen your less-developed coaching skills.

Action Strengths

A simple way to identify your action strengths is to start by listing the activities and tasks you partake in on a day-to-day basis. This exercise is generally referred to as **day-to-day strengths-spotting** (Linley, 2008). Usually, performing these activities and tasks:

- Seem effortless
- Give you a heightened sense of pleasure
- Give you a prolonged focus
- Make you feel energized
- Show a continuous pattern of success

Feedback, comments, or compliments from others is also a crucial part to help give you an indication of what your top five action strengths are. For example, you might hear people say to you:

- Show me how you did that!
- You're the best at...
- This seems so effortless for you.
- When did you learn how to do that?
- You completed that quickly.

While this is helpful, you might also need to sit down with your expert and ask them what you do really well.

Use the tracking sheet to identify your top action strengths, comments you receive from others, and the feeling you have when you use it.

Action strength	How do I feel when I use it?	When do I use it?	What do other people notice when I use it?

Character Strengths

Through scientific study Martin Seligman and his colleagues (2005) identified how an individual's character strengths and virtues can help them to succeed. They identified six core themes, which were separated in 24 universal character strengths. These are outlined below:

- Wisdom and knowledge—Creativity, curiosity, grit, love of learning, perspective
- Courage—Bravery, perseverance, honesty, zest
- Humanity—Love, kindness, social intelligence
- Justice—Teamwork, fairness, leadership
- Temperance—Forgiveness, humility, prudence, self-regulation
- Transcendence—Appreciation of beauty and excellence, gratitude, hope, humor, spirituality

Their work identified that we all have different combinations of the character strengths that make us unique, referred to as signature strengths. Furthermore, they state that when we are using our character strengths, we are the best version of ourselves. To help you identify your top five character strengths, they created the VIA Survey of Character Strengths Test which they have made available through their Authentic Happiness website at www.authentichappiness.com. Once you access the site, find the test under the Questionnaires tab. This test is free to do and worthwhile to help you identify in a scientific way exactly what your character strengths are.

It is important that you answer these questions honestly and accurately, as your answers will help you to identify your top five character strengths.

Character strength	How do I feel when I use it?	When do I use it?	What do other people notice when I use it?

Thinking Strengths

Consider times where you needed to take on new information, plan a route, or solve a particularly challenging situation. Reflect on times when you have been successful in those instances and start to think about the mental process you used to be successful (e.g., you can assess numerical data quickly or remember synonyms for different words).

Here's a list of some different ways of thinking to help you identify how you think when you are at your most productive and have the greatest clarity of thought. It is not exhaustive and you may find you have other ways of thinking that better reflect your strengths.

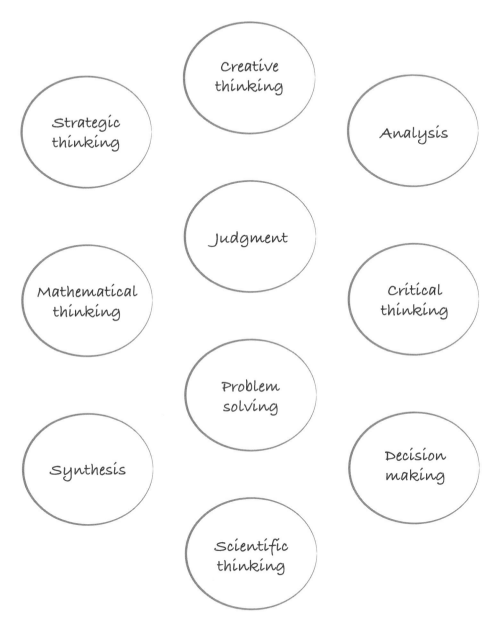

Figure 33 Different thinking strengths

Thinking strength	How do I feel when I use it?	When do I use it?	What do other people notice when I use it?

Now that you have identified your strengths, use your mind-mapping skills to complete the strengths mind map. Add your five strengths in each area to the branches provided. It is important that you regularly refer to your strengths mind map as this will be a source of inspiration and boost confidence when you need it.

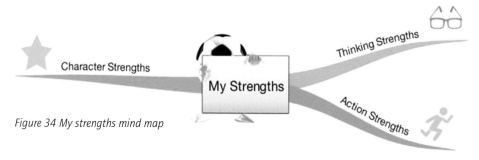

Figure 34 My strengths mind map

3.3 USING YOUR STRENGTHS

Now that you have identified your fifteen strengths, consider how you can use them to purposefully develop your expertise. Consider how strengths can be used in the 3Fs process of purposeful practice (focus, feedback, fix it) by looking at the example below.

Scenario: The aim of this purposeful practice is to develop my session organization.

Element of the 3Fs Identified: Focus	
Strength identified	Thinking strength: Critical thinking
Skill to develop	Session organization: Passing patterns regularly break down
Method for improvement	Using my strength of critical thinking, I can assess the session by asking such questions as: • Why I wasn't successful before? • What did my players need? • What level of learning are they at? • Did they have the required level of technical competency?

Element of the 3Fs Identified: Feedback	
Strength identified	Character strength: Bravery
Skill to develop	Asking for feedback
Method for improvement	Ask for regular feedback during a session from the players and coaches regarding their understanding of the coaching points delivered. From the feedback, I will use my strength of bravery to ask players what they thought of my session and give me feedback.

Element of the 3Fs Identified: Fix It	
Strength identified	Action strength: Demonstrations
Skill to develop	Session organization: Passing pattern breaks down
Method for improvement	Using my action strength of demonstrations, I will perform the skill slowly for them to see all the key elements required.

3.4 DEVELOPMENT OF YOUR SKILLS

Use the tables below to help you consider how you can purposefully use any of your strengths to develop your expertise.

Strength identified	
Skill to develop	
Method for improvement	

Strength identified	
Skill to develop	
Method for improvement	

Strength identified	
Skill to develop	
Method for improvement	

3.5 MAPPING YOUR PERSONAL DEVELOPMENT

Following your record of how you have been using your strengths, start to record any improvements that you have observed in skills you specifically wanted to develop within your coaching. This will help you to develop a clearer understanding of how to use your strengths and how to recognize the impact of your strengths.

Strength	
Improvements observed	

Strength	
Improvements observed	

Strength
Improvements observed

3.6 TIME FOR A RECAP

In this chapter you have learned:

1. About the importance of strengths-based learning and strengths spotting
2. How to identify your action, character, and thinking strengths
3. Ways to use your strengths more purposefully
4. How your strengths have been used to develop purposeful practice

Remember

✔ Your strengths are unique to you and pivotal to your personal development.
✔ Ask others about the strengths you possess.
✔ Keep using and noticing your strengths!

3.7 WHAT TO EXPECT NEXT

The next chapter focuses on how you can develop your reflective skills as a coach practitioner to maximize your learning. This is a key ingredient within the expert coach spectrum.

"To become a critical reflector, reflective practice is an essential learning tool used to question, analyse and evaluate oneself."

4 REFLECTIVE PRACTICE

If there is no process of reflection, we are likely to repeat our mistakes. Just because you have been doing something a long time does not necessarily mean that you have progressed or become any better at it. However, through the process of reflective practice, the intention is to inform and initiate a positive change for future action.

4.1 WHAT IS A REFLECTIVE PRACTICE?

Reflective practice can be defined as a process whereby an individual evaluates and assesses their previous experiences. Their actions and overall characteristics and qualities are considered in a bid to improve future performance. The activity of reflective practice "links experiences and knowledge by providing an opportunity to explore areas of concern in a critical way and to make adjustments based on these reflections" (Farres, 2004, p.1). When approached openly, reflective practice provides you with a clear representation of your practice. It is this that enables us to acknowledge what needs to change—and what we need to be better at.

Furthermore we cannot assume that simply an increase in coaching experience will necessarily enhance the reflective skills of the coach—these must be intentionally developed. Generally, coaches improve and hone their skills through the acquisition of knowledge, shadowing other coaches, and their own personal experiences. In spite of all these experiences, the process of reflective practice is commonly overlooked or inadequately completed for a number of reasons:

- A lack of time (assessing importance)
- Not fully understanding the process (lack of knowledge and guidance)
- Not wanting to accept a lack of understanding in a certain area (avoidance)
- A primary focus on providing feedback and reflection opportunities for the players (prioritizing)

As a result, coaches may lean towards the trial-and-error approach in order to discover what works. However, the sporadic nature of this approach makes reflection a chaotic experience, lacking a clear direction. Hence many coaches disengage from this process after a short period of time.

4.2 BRIDGING THE GAP

In order to develop expertise and improve your effectiveness, reflecting on your behaviors and coaching practice is a key ingredient. For a considerable amount of time, reflective practice has been an essential part of novice development within other professions, such as teaching. However, only recently has the understanding and application of reflective practice been explored within the coaching arena. Nonetheless, coaches still require further guidance to acquire the key skills effectively and accurately to make sense of their experiences and enhance their ability to practice purposefully.

As part of their profession, coaches are constantly trying to cope with new information that is both complex and unique in nature. When a purely rational approach is taken to the reflection process, one will not understand the full picture, as the emotions need to be considered with the experience. When one's emotions are considered with the reflection process, deeper meaning and understanding can be deduced about the given experience. For example, when delivering a new topic, a coach could feel excited because there is another opportunity to learn something different and be stretched, while another coach could feel nervous because they want to remember all the coaching points accurately so that their understanding of the topic is not scrutinized.

Essentially, reflective practice should have a clearly defined role frame (in this case, coaching) to ensure that it is relevant to the expectations and responsibilities of the individual (whether within a school, grassroots, or elite setting). This helps to bring a structure to the reflection process and provides the foundation for understanding how and what you want the reflection to impact upon future delivery.

Within this process is a generic reflection currency which helps to steer and provide a depth of reflective exploration and support the transition to practice more purposefully. This reflection currency takes the form of simple questions such as:

- Who?
- What?
- Where?
- When?
- Why?
- How?
- How much?
- Did I?

These questions provide an appropriate starting point for you to add value to yourself as a coach. When asking yourself the challenging questions, it's important to be completely aware of how your thoughts and feelings affect your actions and judgment. You might find it uncomfortable to ask yourself questions like "Did I know enough about the topic to stretch the players learning?" or "Were the players not fully engaged because my verbal communication was unclear?" Reflective practice is not about being right or wrong but rather being truthful, and is a fundamental part of the journey for coaches to progress through the stages of functioning from novice to expert.

4.3 REFLECTIVE PRACTICE MODEL

Expert coaches regularly partake in reflective practice. Although it might seem to be happening intuitively, the expert coach is following a structured method but at a quicker rate. A helpful framework to make use of is the reflective process outlined by Gibbs (1998). His model clearly defines a six-stage reflective process, which explores the reflective currency in a logical and simple format.

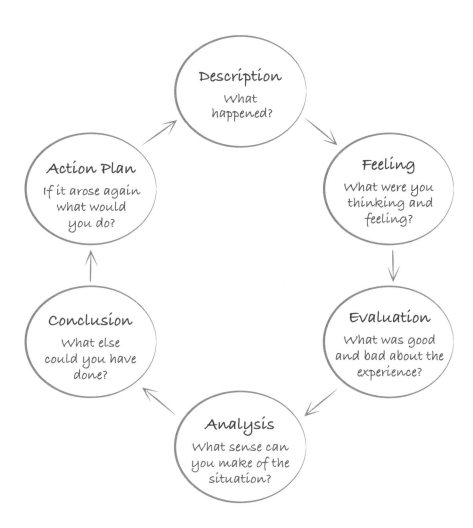

Figure 35 Reflective practice model

Stage 1: Description

This initial stage requires a coach to explain what they are reflecting on. This could be a session, match day, group activity, or discussion. Keeping the information as simple and as relevant as possible is key at this point. Focusing on what happened and who was involved provides a clear enough picture for your reflection to be specific. For example, the "What happened?" could be a session on finishing within the 18-yard area and the "Who was involved?" could be two goalkeepers, four defenders, and four attacking players.

Stage 2: Feelings

The second stage is one that coaches tend to avoid, but it is a key stage in reflective practice. Usually, this type of avoidance occurs because owning our own feelings can make us uncomfortable, especially if they are ones of uncertainty. However, this stage encourages coaches to consider their thought processes and feelings during different moments of the session. This presents coaches with their own emotional landscape throughout the session. Hence, this stage requires coaches to intentionally and truthfully connect with their feelings and thoughts from the experience. This enables coaches to explore areas of genuine vulnerability.

Have a go at asking yourself the following questions:

- How did I feel at the beginning of the session?
- How did I feel during the experience?
- What positively affected my feelings and why was this the case?
- What negatively affected my feelings and why was this the case?
- Did my feelings change throughout the session?

It's important to note that this might not be specifically related to your soccer-specific outcomes of the session. It could be the way a player or a coach spoke to you, or how you felt noticing the way the group integrated a new player. This is helpful as you take into account the whole experience and become even more self-aware as a coach. This enables you to identify and meaningfully understand actions and characteristics which are specific to you. A valid question to ask here would be "How did I feel when using one of my strengths?"

If you have a powerful emotional response during your session, you will often remember more. Research recently conducted by Kensinger (2009) confirmed that negatively and positively charged experiences were remembered more vividly than non-emotive experiences. Furthermore, the research showed that people are more likely to remember negative experiences in greater detail as opposed to positive experiences. For example, after a session, the details of a player forcefully challenging a coach's session organization could be remembered in greater detail than the passage of play for a successful counterattack goal. So it is important to acknowledge your emotional landscape during the session, as it's a clear indicator of when you are in or out of your comfort zone. If you are doing something for the first time, expect to feel uncomfortable. The trick is to persevere in spite of these feelings if you want to become an expert.

Stage 3: Evaluation

In this stage the core aim is to identify the judgments you made and how well you thought the experience went. Historically, the word evaluate originates from the two words "ex" and "value" which translates to "from value." Hence, it should be assumed that every experience a coach has is of intrinsic value and worth and that the significance of the experience should be explored for both soccer specific and non-soccer specific outcomes. Consider the two comments below regarding the same session:

Coach A: *"The players progressed quickly through the ball manipulation part of the practice."*

Coach B: *"Many of the players showed a good level of technical competency in the ball manipulation part of the practice. With excitement, two of the players quickly asked me "What's next, Coach?" This made me feel nervous and stressed as I didn't know how to progress the players onto a more challenging type of ball manipulation skill and therefore moved onto the next part of the practice considerably earlier than planned."*

Of the two evaluations, which one gives you a clearer picture of the coach's experience? Whose comments would enable you to understand where you need to develop your knowledge and improve your planning for the next session? If you're thinking Coach B, then you are spot on! Fundamentally, a few key questions you should be asking yourself in this stage are:

- What judgments did I make and what were the main contributors that influenced my decisions?
- Were my judgments positive or negative?
- How do I feel about the judgments I made?
- How did the players react to the judgments I made?
- What was positive and what was negative about my experience?

Stage 4: Analysis

Through the analysis stage the coach's experience is examined in greater depth. The question "What sense can I make of the situation?" aims to identify a principal aspect or issue of the coaching experience, which had a significant impact and requires investigation for the future. In this stage it is also helpful to compare your experience with additional literature to support future practice. Questions to be considered include:

- What were the main issues identified? Why? How should it work?
- Which ideas are you currently aware of that can help you?
- How can these ideas help you to improve this issue in the future?

Stage 5: Conclusion

At this stage it is important to review the main learning that has taken place. This will involve asking yourself about the key aspects that had the main impact upon your experience and what requires improving. For example it could be that this was the first time you delivered the topic to this group of players or that you had less equipment than expected to deliver your session. This might lead you to ask:

- What else could I have done during this experience?
- What are the main things I have learned from this experience?
- Could I have responded differently at any point?
- Do I require new knowledge?

Stage 6: Action Plan

The final stage considers the actions you need to take to improve your future practice. This is key as the aim each session should be to keep enhancing ways to practice more purposefully.

- What am I going to do differently this time around?
- How can I better prepare?
- Which are the key areas that require developing or planning?
- What are the particular resources I need and how can I get access to them?
- What are the logical steps to follow?

By asking these questions you will be able to recognize where you might need more information, understanding, or skill. This will in turn prompt you to seek guidance from your expert mentor and access the necessary resources to support your future practice. Also remember that you can use your personal strengths to enhance the effectiveness of your reflective practice as well.

Times for Reflection

As described and identified by Schon (1983), the process of reflection can take place in two ways, either reflection in action or reflection on action. Simply, reflection in action involves reflecting and immediately acting upon an experience while it is taking place. Conversely, reflection on action works by reflecting on an experience after it has happened (such as Gibbs' model outlined previously).

Reflection in Action

This is the most challenging of the two types of reflection for the coach, as it requires the coach to observe, consolidate, and decide on an immediate and appropriate action to positively impact their players. This is an essential tool to use within coaching, as the nature of the job requires thinking on your feet. An obvious example of this is making a substitution.

This type of reflection is dynamic in its nature as surprising and unexpected events can occur at any time. Soccer constantly presents novel situations for the coach, which challenges their knowing in action (knowledge previously acquired in other or related experiences) and ability to appropriately apply it. Coaches will find that in-the-moment decisions will have to be made to try and find what works best at that point in time.

Reflection on Action

Alternatively, reflection on action focuses on reflecting after the experience has taken place. It is important to note that reflection occurs regardless of the conscious decision to do so. Nevertheless a more structured approach will help to organize your thoughts, feelings, and actions in a cohesive manner and enhance your capacity to be more effective in subsequent practices. Therefore, the most important aspect of this part is for the coach to:

1. Consolidate and make connections between what was planned (theory) and what was delivered (practice)

2. Make sense of and identify clear conclusions and development areas from the complexity of the coaching process

3. Be better informed to engage in more purposeful practice.

4.4 REMEMBER TO INVOLVE OTHERS

When reflecting it's important to note that involving those within the experience will be of benefit. It will help you to piece the whole experience together as they will consider and present aspects of the experience that you have missed, assumed, or misinterpreted. These key figures include:

- Coach to peer coach
- Coach to expert coach
- Coach to player

Overall, the reflection process has to be self-driven to be an effective process. As an individual you have to take responsibility for and accept your own action or inaction. Fundamentally, you must own what you do.

4.5 TIME FOR A RECAP

In this chapter you have learned:

1. The importance of reflective practice to develop expertise
2. How to reflect through Gibbs' six stages of reflective practice
3. Reflection in action and reflection on action

Remember

✔ The more you reflect the more effective you will be
✔ Involve others in your reflection process
✔ Act on your reflections

4.6 WHAT TO EXPECT NEXT

Now it's time to look at how you the coach can apply similar principles you have learned throughout this book to your players. If you practice purposefully then teaching your players how to do so will enhance their development potential.

"Deep practice is built on a paradox: Struggling in certain targeted ways – operating at the edges of your ability, where you make mistakes makes you smarter. We think of effortless performance as desirable, but it's really a terrible way to learn."

(Coyle, 2009, p. 18)

APPLICATION OF THE PRINCIPLES: DEVELOPING YOUR CRITICAL EYE

The primary focus of the book has been on developing yourself as a coach. However there are of course some important applications of these techniques and principles that you can apply to develop your players.

The assumption has been that the longer your players train the better they will become (e.g., the 10,000-hour rule). However, this must be challenged, given what you now know about developing expertise and how to practice with purpose. It should be clear to you that if you design sessions for your players that are not in accordance with the 3F principles (see chapter 2) and are not focused on each individual's developmental needs, you will not be able to develop expert players. It is also important that you create a coaching environment in which the players understand the importance of purposeful practice and that they use the principles every time they train.

The application of these principles below will enable you to create purposeful training:

1. Create clear collaborative goals and intentions with your players.
2. Ensure you stay focused and present when you are coaching. Notice and assess the detail.
3. Give feedback effectively to notice what needs to change.
4. Help solve the problems and find a solution.

5.1 COLLABORATIVE PLAYER GOALS

Setting goals has long been part of coaches' work. However, too often, the player has not been involved. In order for this to be effective it should be a two-way interactive process between player and coach. There are of course different time framed goals: short term, medium term, and long term. Use the mastery approach model to help players set the right types of objectives. You can assist here by checking that they fulfill requirements appropriately. Having this discussion will also help you to understand what is important to your players. Often the goals that are set seem to be unrelated to training, and are focused on game situations where players have less control over their environment. This is problematic as players are missing opportunities to maximize their efforts and increase their learning during training. If you ask players "What did you achieve in training?," they will often not be able to answer you. This shows that training is not purposeful, so it becomes simply something that they participate in.

Key Steps

1. Ensure that players set their own goals and intentions.
2. Ensure that in every training session you ask the players what their intentions are and ensure that these are very focused and specific.
3. Ensure that you ask at the end of training if their intentions were achieved. If so, ask "How?" And if not, ask how can they fix it.

Notice, Analyze, and Assess

The skill of an expert coach lies in their ability to be able to give appropriate feedback to their players. However, if you are not able to recognize the detail in each movement as it is performed by your players, it will render the feedback ineffective. Part of this process is to be able to recognize at what stage of learning and skill development each player is performing. Fitts and Posner's (1967) model of the stages of skill development is a useful tool to help you do this. This is important because not only does it differentiate between players' skills levels, but it also provides a mechanism to work effectively within each stage to ensure that players can make the transition to the autonomous stage. This is dependent upon the level of instruction that players receive, as well as the quality and frequency of the feedback given by the coach.

5.2 STAGES OF SKILL DEVELOPMENT

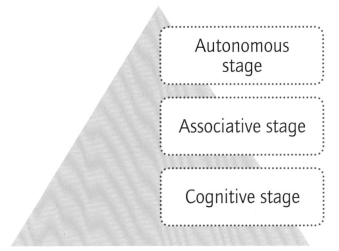

Figure 36 Three stages of skill development

Cognitive Stage

This is the first stage of skill development and is characterized by lots of errors and inconsistencies in the movement patterns. The movement will often appear to be clunky and awkward. If a movement has several parts to it, they may be able to perform some parts better than others. Performing the skill will require all-consuming attention and effort.

The most effective coaching strategy for players at this stage of development is to ensure that training tasks are structured to ensure that players get early success which will keep them engaged and motivated. A simple example of this is to introduce the skill with each player working on their own first, then moving on to paired work, and finally adding in more players. At this stage it is important that there is frequent repetition with detailed feedback on the specifics of the movement. You will have to consider how you demonstrate the skill to ensure the player understands exactly what is expected of them. Only then can they have a clear mental picture of the skill. The errors that will occur are useful signposts for the learner if you notice and use them constructively. So if a skill doesn't work, you can ask questions such as "Where were your hips, feet, or shoulders?," "How did it feel?," and "Where was your attention?" By asking these type of questions you are helping the player become more aware of their own body in the movement, and they can begin to become their own error detector. Often in soccer these details are missed and only the outcome (i.e., where the ball went) is commented upon. This is a missed opportunity for players to anchor core techniques and fundamental movements. It is also important that feedback is positive in nature as this helps to facilitate the players' confidence as well as feeling a sense of achievement. So if the skill is messy, you can acknowledge to the player that they are learning and they are not there...YET.

Associative Stage

The second stage is characterized by movements that have more fluidity and control. The movements will still have errors but these are becoming less frequent. They are now able to increase the speed of simple movements and combine movements together. Players are now beginning to be able to error detect for themselves, especially if in the cognitive stage they were given lots of detailed feedback. Players will need less narrow focus to execute the skill which will give them spare attentional capacity to engage with their environment.

The most effective coaching strategy for this stage is still to maintain lots of repetition of the movement to ensure that the mind develops accurate motor schemas which creates the synchronization of mind and body. Continue the use of the reflective questioning to encourage error detection and anchoring of correct technique. For example, if a player performs a movement well you can ask "What did you notice about how you did it?,"

"How did it feel?," and "What did you do to make it work?" For players, recognizing how they achieved success is important. This will enable them to feel confident that they can do it again which in turn enhances their feeling of competence—a critical component of intrinsic motivation.

Similarly if something does not work it should simply be viewed as an opportunity to learn. We should expect mistakes and understand how they create learning opportunities. The key here is how we maintain an open and emotionally neutral response when we are giving feedback to players. At this stage of learning it is critical that the coach pays constant attention to detail and correction required to complete the skill efficiently and effectively; the value of such specificity cannot be overlooked.

So using questions such as "What did you notice about how you did it?," "What needs to change?," "How did it feel?," and "What can you do to make it work?" will encourage players to notice the detail themselves which is important if they are to be able to make the transition into the next stage. You can also give detailed feedback to the players about how they are executing any movement patterns. Sometimes you can also engage other players to give feedback to each other. This will help the players understand what is needed and by recognizing it in others this will help cement their understanding.

Autonomous Stage

The final stage is where the movement can be performed with ease and requires little attention. The movement will appear fluid and smooth. The consistency of the movement is now in evidence. The automated simple movements can now be combined with others to create complex sequences. This can only happen if the player has correctly refined all of the inherent sub-routines and building blocks required for efficient execution. If they have not received the detailed feedback in the cognitive and associative stages they may never progress to this stage. At this stage the player will have a well-anchored motor schema that they can use in different situations. This defines the skilled player who has a library of autonomous skills and knows exactly which one to use in any given situation.

The coach needs to continue to challenge the player to recognize their own mistakes to help them become really efficient error detectors. They should be experts of their own bodies and movement patterns. If players do not understand why something worked or didn't work, they will not be able to become experts with a library of automated skills. Again, view mistakes as opportunities to grow and develop. Consider this: "Deep practice is built on a paradox: struggling in certain targeted ways—operating at the edges of your ability, where you make mistakes—makes you smarter. We think of effortless performance as desirable, but it's really a terrible way to learn" (Coyle, 2009 pg. 18). So if you are to embrace the notion of learning and development by ensuring that you notice and analyze effectively, you will be able to help your players move into the autonomous stage for all of their skills.

It is also important to understand that a player may be at different stages of development for different skills. For example, a young player might be at the associative stage for a punch pass, but at the cognitive stage for crossing. A further complication within soccer is that the stages of development may also be different in the different contexts. So for example a player could execute a punch pass consistently 10/10 times when they are doing it unopposed, but this might not be the case once some interference is introduced such as another player closing them down. The question then becomes where are they in relation to the stage of learning now? Use the following table to assess some of your players in relation to the stage of learning that they are at for different skills.

Skill Assessment

Figure 37 Skill assessment

Once you have identified their stage of learning you can ensure that you create training plans that are appropriate for their stage of learning. For example, if a player has a skill that is at the cognitive stage of learning, do not expect them to be able to execute it efficiently in an opposed game situation. It is only when a skill is at the autonomous stage of learning that you can expect that. Given the rules of skill development it is only through repetition with detailed feedback that they will be able to progress. Do not expect this to happen if you never do this in training. In the beginning you may have to manage your expectations and set intentions in relation to part of the skill, for example their foot patterns.

Building the Library

In essence it is your job as the coach to help players build a big library of autonomous skills. It is critical that you understand the fundamental skills that underpin each ball skill. So for example, if a player's jump is inefficient and inconsistent, they don't yet have the fundamental skill to be able to jump and head the ball. They will need to develop this first before they move onto the ball skill. If this is not done, then it is likely that the skill of heading will not develop past the cognitive stage. In a fast-moving sport like soccer, the fundamental skills must be automated when players are in the least demanding context (i.e., unopposed training). So when you are analyzing and assessing players' skills, notice the context and ask yourself if this then changes the level of automation. For example, it might look like this:

Player X: Heading

Context	Stage of development
Unopposed (training)	Autonomous
With interference (training)	Autonomous
Opposed (training	Associative
Unopposed (match)	Associative
With interference (match) from teammate	Associative
Opposed (match)	Associative

By doing this detailed analysis of your players, you will have a depth of knowledge that will enable you to create the most effective training programs to meet the developmental needs of your players.

The last aspect to consider when assessing your players is the psychological context which can change how skills are executed. For example, the state of the game can have an influence – if a team is winning easily, then skills in the associative stage may appear automatic. However this might not be the case if they are losing and anxiety is being experienced. The same can be true if the skill is being performed in different areas of the pitch – if it is in your own half, then skills might appear more automated than when they are being performed in the opposition's half. You might also have to consider if the execution of skills changes depending upon who is watching. This process can be helped through your understanding of visual awareness.

5.3 VISUAL AWARENESS

Given that the game is now played at faster speeds, the requirement for athletes to anticipate and respond to various forms of visual information at a quicker rate is now even more imperative. This subsequently has a significant impact on the soccer coach who has to anticipate, recognize, and prioritize the choices the players have to make at a quicker rate during training and match scenarios. Therefore, within the reflection-in-action aspect, there is an increasing importance for coaches to analyze their own ability to notice and identify what is actually being performed by the players in relation to the session outcome and which areas need more deliberate visual attention than others.

It is helpful for coaches to understand the difference between visual awareness for the coach in comparison to the player. Specifically, the player needs to both recognize the situation and perform the physical action required simultaneously, while the coach needs to recognize the situation and in turn identify the physical action required for the player to perform. Thus, as the observer, the coach must consider whether the perceived physical action they believe the player should perform is realistic to the situation.

Giving Quality Feedback

Feedback always needs to be referenced back to the goals and intentions set for that session. Feedback that lacks specificity becomes meaningless and of little real value to the player. It is also important that feedback is aligned to the stage of learning that a player is at. Try using the sandwich approach outlined below as this has been shown to be very effective in maximizing children's learning. Players are more likely to be receptive to and follow feedback when they do not feel judged or threatened, and are instead provided with detailed feedback on what needs to be fixed. This will help them engage in training in a more purposeful way. You also need to be aware of and manage your own emotions. The manner in which you communicate will let you know how well you are doing this. So if you are angry, you will not be effective in your use of feedback as the emotion of anger changes your perception and you will never be getting the whole picture.

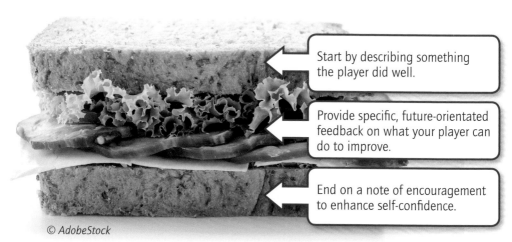

Start by describing something the player did well.

Provide specific, future-orientated feedback on what your player can do to improve.

End on a note of encouragement to enhance self-confidence.

© AdobeStock

Figure 38 Sandwich approach to feedback

As previously stated, the use of questions can be a very effective way for you to empower the player to reflect on their own performance. Of course they will need guidance in this process, but you want them to be able to detect their own errors and be able to find a solution. Feedback that is future oriented is especially helpful for players in the cognitive stage as it recognizes that they aren't there YET. However, that doesn't mean they won't master it in the future if they follow your guided feedback.

After a training session or game, it is really effective to ask your players to identify any aspects of their performance that went well. This is very important because coaches often only use the lens of pathology (i.e., what went wrong). Constantly hearing this can be very demoralizing and significantly affect self-confidence. It is also important that players are able to feel that they created good moments and that they can repeat them. So consider using this approach:

- What went really well?
- How did you make it happen?
- How can you repeat it?

You create the learning environment for your players through your feedback. Players are dependent upon you to help them move through the stages of skill development which in turn helps them become expert players.

Finding the Solution

The final part of the process of developing your critical eye is to be able to find effective solutions to skill development problems. However, you can only do this if you have already done stages 1, 2, and 3. Finding solutions doesn't necessarily mean that the players have to try harder, sometimes it is about doing something in a different way. So if it isn't working and players aren't developing their skills, you have to ask yourself what you can do to make training more effective. Sometimes it is easy for coaches to assume that if there isn't any development the fault must lie with the player—this isn't always the case. You need to be prepared to ask yourself what you should be doing better to enhance their learning. It can also be helpful to get players to contribute to finding a solution because what works for them might not have worked for you or you might not have come up with the same solution. The solutions or fix-it aspects of purposeful practice are then fed back into the process and become the focus for the next training session. The cycle becomes continuous and now you have embedded purposeful practice into everything that you and your players do.

5.4 SCHEMATIC FOR DEVELOPING YOUR CRITICAL EYE

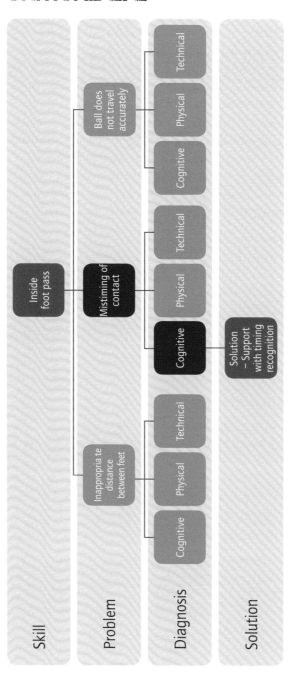

Figure 39 Skill diagnostic for unopposed training: Associative stage

The schematic diagram above illustrates the process that you will need to go through in order to develop your critical eye. The less experience you have the more important it is for you to go deliberately through each of the steps:

- Identify the problem.
- Find a diagnosis.
- Create the solution.

As you become more expert you will be able to recognize quickly what the problem is and how to solve it. Indeed the critical eye is a factor that separates expert coaches from novices. Often the diagnosis doesn't consider all aspects of performance and essentially only highlights the technical aspects. However, often the problems can be cognitive or psychological in nature which will of course require a very different solution. While this may look like a long-winded, slow process, it quickly becomes embedded in the way you coach and is easy to use in practice. It does, however, require you to think consciously differently. Through this process you will be able to give really effective, focused feedback which will help your players reach their full potential.

5.5 TIME FOR A RECAP

In this chapter you have learned:

1. The importance of setting clear intentions and goals
2. How to identify the stages of skill acquisition
3. Ways to use your strengths more purposefully
4. How to use skills diagnostics to find coaching solutions

Remember

- ✔ Setting clear intentions with your players will enhance purposeful practice.
- ✔ Regularly engage in forward-focused feedback activities.
- ✔ Keep working on building your players' technical library.

CONCLUSION

The intention of this book has been to develop your understanding of how to become an expert coach using the technique of mind mapping to help you. Like learning anything new and different it will take time and an investment of effort before you can fully reap the rewards. But as you will have read, perseverance is always at the heart of success, and hopefully this book will be your companion for many years to come. Shape it as you want, create new aspects as you go. Your journey will be unique and different from everyone else's which makes it very special.

Hopefully you are now able to recognize what you want to do differently. Change is a good thing when it is something that we have identified to help us move toward excellent practice. This is an important way to consider your personal growth. Taking time to gain perspective is often neglected as we get immersed in the everyday and we can find ourselves repeating actions that don't actually develop our potential. Maybe we should all take a leaf out of Mark Zuckerberg and Bill Gates' books; they regularly schedule reflection and thinking time into their days and look what they were able to accomplish. The key to success is being purposeful—and it doesn't happen by accident. It takes time and effort, the foundation for your own personal development.

What we would like for you to have achieved on this journey is a better understanding of your current level of expertise and your coaching skills. Engaging in an honest appraisal of your skills is your starting point. Hopefully you will have tried the exercises throughout the book, and now have a clearer understanding of yourself. It is also anticipated that you are beginning to become skillful at using mind maps to help you in a range of different situations. By regularly using these effective tools you will be able to fast track your learning and find more effective ways to problem solve. Ensuring that you are aware of the process to develop expertise through the 3Fs (focus, feedback, and fix it) will allow you to become much more productive and maximize your learning opportunities. By doing this you will be taking control of your own learning, rather than it happening accidentally. It is worth being reminded of that important element identified by Liz Beaty (1997) when she said that "whilst we all learn from experience, more and more experience does not guarantee more and more learning." So if there is no reflection and purposeful development, the outcome of ten years of coaching may not equate to ten years of learning about coaching but may simply be only one year repeated ten times. So in essence you have stood still and have not actually enhanced your expertise.

Understand what it means to be an expert—take control of your own learning!

All being well you will be doing things differently and using all your available resources to help you throughout the process. Being an expert coach involves doing and thinking in a distinctive way. It is about creating your own library of knowledge that is readily available. Throughout this book you have learned different ways of using your mind-mapping process to understand how you think. Importantly, understanding these principles will provide you with the guidance to maximize your cognitive processes. Then through regular and intentional practice and reflection, you will be able to gradually refine the way your brain:

- Formulates new concepts
- Acquires new information
- Recalls information

These cognitive functions are the cornerstone of expert thinking and enable you to quickly solve problems, and use effective strategies to maximize the development of your players. This book will also have helped you understand your unique inner resources—your strengths which you can draw upon whenever you need them. As previously discussed, the coaches' challenge is that if 90% of meaningful learning takes place on the job, then how do you know you're maximizing these opportunities? By knowing your action, character, and thinking strengths, you can harness them to your advantage. So by confidently owning what you're good at, developing your coaching expertise should become easier and more rewarding.

The aim of this book was to provide you with simple but effective and interactive learning tools to develop your coaching expertise. With the six fundamental coaching components addressed throughout this book, the tools to identify, assess, and implement your personal coaching needs are now at your fingertips. Now, when you participate in future learning within informal and formal settings you can use this newly formed personal resource to independently support you to:

- Accurately evaluate your current coaching skills

- Understand that your own soccer memory bank created a mental library that you can effectively access and add to

- Enhance, develop, and acquire specific coaching expertise

- Identify your personal strengths in order to help support the development of your expertise

- Advance your reflective practice skills

- Apply these principles to those you are coaching

Enjoy your personal coaching journey so that you and your players can reap the rewards of your expert skills and knowledge.

BIBLIOGRAPHY

Adodo, S.O. (2013). Effect of mind-mapping as a self-regulated learning strategy on students' achievement in basic science and technology. *Mediterranean Journal of Social Sciences, 4(6), 163-172.*

Beaty, L. (1997). *Developing Your Teaching Through Reflective Practice.* Birmingham: SEDA.

Brewerton, P. (2011). Using strengths to drive career success. *Strategic HR Review,* 10(6), pp. 5-10.

Bridgeman, G., Hendry, D., Start, L. (1975). Failure to detect displacement of visual world during saccadic eye movements. *Vision Research, 15,* 719-722.

Buzan, T. (1991). Executive excellence. *Mind Mapping,* 8.8, 3.

Buzan, T. (1996). *The Mind Map Book: How to Use Radiant Thinking to Maximise Your Brain's Untapped Potential.* New York: Plume.

Coyle, D. (2009). *The Talent Code: Greatness Isn't Born, It's Grown, Here's How.* New York: Bantam Books.

Critchell, M., Bosma, J.J.D., and Granger, K. (2008). *Game Vision in Football: Theory and Practice to Improve Game Sense.* London: The Football Garage.

Cushion, C.J., Armour, K.M., and Jones, R.L. (2003). Coach education and continuing professional development: experience and learning to coach. *Quest, 55,* 215-230.

Ericsson, A., and Poole, R. (2016). *Peak: Secrets from the New Science of Expertise.* UK: Bodley Head.

Ericsson, K.A., Prietula, M.J., and Cokely, E.T. (2007). The making of an expert. *Harvard Business Review: Managing People, July-August 2007 Issue.*

FA Learning. (2010). *The Future Game Grassroots: The Football Association Technical Guide for Young Player Development – Philosophy.* Leeds: FA Learning.

Farres, L. G. (2004). Becoming a better coach through reflective practice. *BC Coach's Perspective, 6,* 1-5.

Henderson, J.M. (2003). Human gaze control during real-world scene perception. *Trends in Cognitive Sciences, 7*(11), 498-504.

Irwin, D., and Brockmole, J.R. (2004). Suppressing where but not what. The effects of saccades on norsal and ventral stream visual processing. *Psychological Science, 15*(7), 467-473.

Kensinger, E.A. (2009). Remembering the details: effects of emotion. *Emot Rev, 1*(2), 99-113.

Linley, A. (2008). *Average to A+: Realising Strengths in Yourself and Others.* United Kingdom: CAPP Press.

McLeod, P. (1994). Perceptual motor co-ordination. In M.W. Eysenck (Ed.), *Blackwell Dictionary of Cognitive Psychology* (pp. 262-264). Oxford: Blackwell.

Olurinola, O., and Tayo, O. (2015). Colour in learning: its effect on the retention rate of graduate students. *Journal of Education and Practice, 6*(14), 1-5.

Paris, S.G., and Paris, A.H. (2001). Classroom applications of research on self-regulated learning. *Educational Psychologist, 36*(2), 89-101.

Schon, D. (1983). *The Reflective Practitioner: How professionals think in action.* London: Temple Smith.

Vickers, J.N. (2007). *Perception, Cognition, and Decision Training: The Quiet Eye in Action.* Illinois: Human Kinetics.

Wade, G. (2016). *Coaching Better Every Season: A Year-Round System for Athlete Development and Program Success.* Illinois: Human Kinetics.

Wiman, M., Salmoni, A.W., and Hall, C.R. (2010). An examination of the definition and development of expert coaching. *International Journal of Coaching Science, 4*(2), pp. 37-60.

APPENDIX: TERMINOLOGY

Throughout the book there will be generic terms used with which you may not be familiar. The definitions of these terminologies are outlined below:

coaching point — A coaching point is a short piece of information given to an individual player or group of players to help improve technical, tactical, physical, or social performance within a practice. Coaching points are relevant to the topic of the session and the specific activities outlined within the session. A coach generally delivers this when a player performs an action incorrectly or where there is an immediate opportunity to extend learning.

positive learning environment — This is a situation where the players feel comfortable, confident, and safe to share their thoughts and feelings in an individual or collective group scenario. This could be related to actions, discussions, or observations where pre-, during and post-instruction feedback is shared coach to player and player to player. Each individual should be able to engage with an activity where they can thrive and make mistakes, with both encouragement and guidance provided in a clear manner where open dialogue is always available. It has been shown that players learn best in a positive environment and the coach is responsible for creating it.

session plan — This is a planned and organized description of clearly defined learning outcomes that are directly related to and achieved through progressive activities. Within these activities, opportunities are provided to practice the learning outcomes as an individual and as a group. The session plan also identifies the duration of each activity, the coaching points relevant for the topic explored within the session, and the structure of the activities.

CREDITS

Interior Figures: © Temisan Williams and Misia Gervis, unless otherwise noted

Cover Design: Katerina Georgieva

Interior Design and Layout: Annika Naas

Managing Editor: Elizabeth Evans

Copyediting: Anne Rumery